5   nt

50 *Hikes*

in Vermont

Walks, Hikes, and Overnights in the Green Mountain State

Sixth Edition

THE GREEN MOUNTAIN CLUB
Dave Hardy, Editor

Backcountry Guides

Woodstock, Vermont

An Invitation to the Reader

Over time trails can be rerouted and signs and landmarks altered. If you find that changes have occurred on the routes described in this book, please let us know so that corrections may be made in future editions. The author and publisher also welcome other comments and suggestions. Address all correspondence to:

Editor, 50 Hikes™ Series
Backcountry Guides
P.O. Box 748
Woodstock, VT 05091

Library of Congress Cataloging-in-Publication Data

50 hikes in Vermont : walks, hikes, and overnights in the Green Mountain State / the Green Mountain Club. -- 6th ed.
    p. cm.
  Previous ed. entered under Lindemann, Bob.
  ISBN 0-88150-538-2
    1. Hiking--Vermont--Guidebooks. 2. Vermont--Guidebooks. I. Title: Fifty hikes in Vermont. II. Green Mountain Club.

GV199.42. 7V4 L55 2003
917.43'0444--dc21
                        2002038544

Series design by Glenn Suokko
Trail overlays by Richard Widhu and Mapping Specialists, Ltd., Madison, WI
Cover photograph by Alden Pellett

Managing Editor: Dave Hardy
Volunteer Editors: Bill Clark, Cheryl McQueen

© 2003 by The Green Mountain Club

Sixth Edition

Published by Backcountry Guides,
a division of The Countryman Press
P.O. Box 748
Woodstock, VT 05091

Distributed by W.W. Norton & Company Inc.
500 Fifth Avenue
New York, NY 10110

Printed in the United States of America
10 9 8 7 6 5 4 3 2 1

ACKNOWLEDGMENTS

Many interested parties made this book possible, including the following individuals who reviewed the hikes in person and in print: Jeff Nugent, Bill Clark, Katie Antos-Ketcham, Pete Antos-Ketcham, Melissa Green, Dave Iverson, Cat Eich, Bruce Scofield, Beth Dugger, Scott Christiansen, Marge Fish, Jane Coffey, Seth Coffey, Herb Ogden, Mary Lou Recor, Randall Travis, Megan Epler-Wood, Chris Hanna, Reidun Nuquist, Andrew Nuquist, Susan Shea, Kevin Harty, Susan Sakash, Matthew Shannon, Greg Western, and Carol Gregory.

50 Hikes in Vermont at a Glance

HIKE	LOCATION
1. Mount Olga	East of Wilmington
2. Prospect Rock (Manchester)	East of Manchester
3. White Rocks/Ice Beds Trail	Near Wallingford
4. Harmon Hill	East of Bennington
5. Haystack Mountain	West of Wilmington
6. Bald Mountain	North of Townshend Village
7. Antone Mountain	West of Rupert
8. Bromley Mountain	East of Manchester
9. Little Rock Pond and Green Mountain	East of Danby
10. Okemo Mountain	West of Ludlow
11. Stratton Pond	Betweeen Arlington and W. Wardsboro
12. Mount Ascutney	West of Ascutney
13. Griffith Lake and Baker Peak	South of Danby
14. Stratton Mountain	Between Arlington and W. Wardsboro
15. Little Rock Pond and Clarendon Gorge	Between Danby and Clarendon
16. Robert Frost Trail	East of Ripton
17. Texas Falls	West of Hancock
18. Quechee Gorge	East of Woodstock
19. Mount Horrid's Great Cliff	At Brandon Gap
20. Dear Leap Overlook	At Sherburne Pass
21. Mount Independence	West of Orwell
22. Mount Tom	Near Woodstock
23. Rattlesnake Point	Northeast of Brandon
24. Snake Mountain	South of Addison
25. Pico Peak	At Sherburne Pass

DISTANCE (miles)	VERTICAL RISE (feet)	DIFFICULTY	VIEWS	GOOD FOR KIDS	CAMPING NEARBY	GOOD FOR WINTER	NOTES
1.6	500	E/M	★	★	★	★	x-c skiing; snowshoeing; fire tower
3.0	1,100	S	★		★	★	Rock outcrop over ravine
2.0	460	E	★	★		★	Snowshoeing
3.4	1,265	M	★		★	★	Snowshoeing
4.8	1,020	M	★			★	Snowshoeing; parking difficult in winter
3.4	1,100	M	★		★	★	Snowshoeing
5.0	890	M		★	★	★	x-c skiing; snowshoeing; limited views
5.0	890	M	★				Observation tower
7.0	960	M/S	★		★	★	x-c skiing
6.0	1,950	M	★			★	Snowshoeing; fire tower
7.8	660	M			★	★	x-c skiing; snowshoeing
5.8	2,060	S	★		★		Views from rock outcrops
8.2	2,340	S	★		★		Open summit ledges
9.3	1,910	M/S	★		★	★	Strenuous snowshoeing; fire tower
15.0	3,100	E/M	★		★		Overnight hike; need 2 cars
1.0	120	E	★	★		★	Snowshoeing; x-c skiing
1.2	160	E	★		★		Waterfalls
1.6	250	E	★	★			170-foot deep gorge
1.4	620	M	★		★	★	Snowshoeing; peregrine falcons
2.0	520	E	★	★	★	★	Snowshoeing
2.5	200	E/M		★			Interpretive center; historical interest
3.5	600	M	★	★			x-c skiing
3.9	1,160	M	★		★	★	Snowshoeing
3.5	980	M	★		★		Mountain was once an island
5.8	1,800	M	★		★		Open summit ledges

50 Hikes in Vermont at a Glance

HIKE	LOCATION
26. Mount Abraham	East of Bristol
27. Mount Roosevelt	West of Granville
28. Bread Loaf Mountain	South of Lincoln
29. Mount Grant	South of Lincoln
30. Monroe Skyline	Between Lincoln and Appalachian Gaps
31. Appalachian Trail	Near Woodstock
32. Owl's Head	East of Marshfield
33. Hires and Sensory Trails	Near Huntington
34. Prospect Rock	West of Johnson
35. Mount Philo	North of Ferrisburg
36. Black Creek and Maquam Creek Trails	North of Swanton
37. Little River History Loop	West of Waterbury
38. Stowe Pinnacle	East of Stowe Village
39. Bluff Mountain	Near Island Pond
40. Spruce Mountain	South of Plainfield
41. Elmore Mountain and Balanced Rock	South of Morrisville
42. Mount Pisgah	South end of Lake Willoughby
43. Jay Peak	East of Montgomery
44. Hubbard Park	In Montpelier
45. Mount Hunger	East of Waterbury Center
46. Mount Monadnock	South of Canaan
47. Sterling Pond and Elephant's Head	At Smuggler's Notch
48. Mount Mansfield	North of Stowe
49. Camel's Hump	West of Waterbury
50. Hazen's Notch to Eden Crossing	North of Eden Mills

DISTANCE (miles)	VERTICAL RISE (feet)	DIFFICULTY	VIEWS	GOOD FOR KIDS	CAMPING NEARBY	GOOD FOR WINTER	NOTES
5.8	2,500	S	★		★		Busy summit during fall foliage season
6.8	2,100	M	★		★		Vista just north of summit
8.6	2,235	S	★		★		Highest point in Breadloaf Wilderness
8.4	1,960	S	★		★		Ascend along mountain stream
12.2	2,535	M	★		★		Overnight hike; need 2 cars
22.3	5,160	S	★		★		Overnight hike; need 2 cars
0.5	160	E	★	★	★	★	x-c skiing, snowshoeing
1.25	200	E	★	★		★	Snowshoeing; museum and interpretative center
1.6	540	E	★	★		★	Snowshoeing
2.0	650	M	★	★	★	★	x-c skiing; snowshoeing
2.7	25	E		★			Wildlife refuge trails
3.5	880	E/M		★			Ghost town; some x-c skiing
2.8	1,520	M	★			★	Snowshoeing
3.4	1,080	M	★			★	Snowshoeing
4.5	1,180	M	★			★	Strenuous snowshoe; fire tower
4.5	1,470	M	★		★	★	Snowshoeing; fire tower
4.0	1,590	M	★				Peregrine falcons on cliff over Lake Willoughby
3.4	1,680	M	★			★	Open summit with tramway station
5.75	374	M	★			★	Snowshoeing; x-c skiing
4.4	2,290	M/S	★			★	Strenuous snowshoe to open summit
4.8	2,108	S	★				Fire tower
6.8	1,780	S	★		★		High mountain pond
6.0	3,200	S	★		★		Highest peak in Vermont
7.4	2,645	S	★		★	★	Very strenuous snowshoe
10.0	3,043	S	★		★		Fire tower; overnight hike; need 2 cars

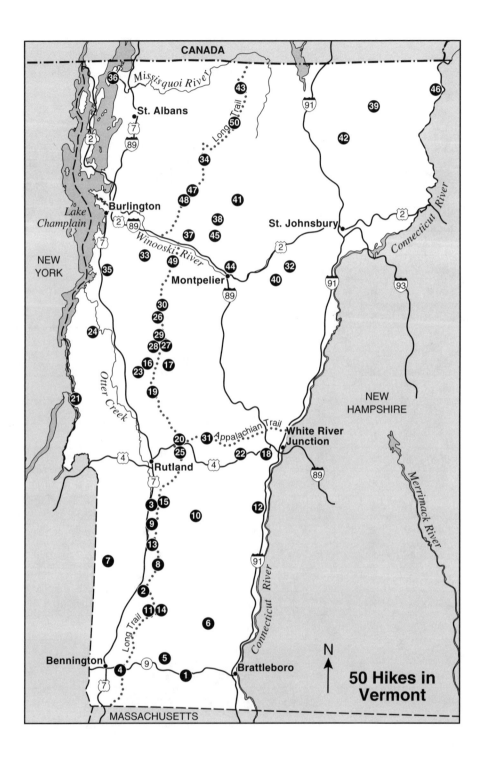

CONTENTS

Foreword to the Sixth Edition

Some things get better with age. *50 Hikes in Vermont* is one of those things.

This sixth edition retains the beloved classic hikes from past editions and adds a generous sprinkling of worthy new suggestions.

Allow me to introduce the sixth edition's editor-in-chief, Dave Hardy. Dave is the Green Mountain Club's director of field programs. When I first came to work at the club in 1998, somebody told me that the best way to update GMC's comprehensive guidebook, *The Long Trail Guide*, would be to "download Dave's brain." We have been trying ever since.

Dave is the son of Gerald and Sue Hardy, renowned as the original authors of *50 Hikes in Connecticut*; he has taken over as the editor of that popular collection. As an avid recreational hiker and longtime volunteer trail maintainer, Dave offers a seasoned eye. He is also a former nuclear submarine engineer (this has nothing to do with this book, but is too interesting to leave out). Anyhow, if Dave says, "This is one of the fifty best hikes in the state!", you know it is going to be a great hike.

Furthermore, he didn't start from scratch. On the contrary, the editors of the past several editions, Bob Lindemann and Mary Deaett, did an extraordinary job. Their efforts to compile and describe most of the hikes in this book were a labor of love for the Green Mountains and typify the spirit of volunteerism that keeps Vermont's hiking trails open for use. We owe them our gratitude.

Although edited by Dave (who is now a professional trail geek), this edition remains fundamentally a volunteer project. Each hike has been walked, checked, and written up by one or more of the volunteers listed in the acknowledgments. As with most things at the Green Mountain Club, updating *50 Hikes* has been a team effort.

Because you are holding this book in your hands, you are already engaged in a relationship with the mountains of Vermont. It is but a small step from enjoying one or more of the trails described in these pages to active involvement in the Green Mountain Club.

Since 1910, the club has been Vermont's leading organization for trail building, hiking trail advocacy, and hiker education. The 445 miles of the Long Trail System (that is, 270 miles along the spine of the Green Mountains from Massachusetts to Quebec, plus side trails) represent nearly half of all the miles of public hiking trails in Vermont. This collection has a similar ratio: roughly half of the hikes are on the Long Trail, the other half are scattered east and west of the Green Mountain ridgeline in all corners of Vermont.

One thing that binds all of the trails together is the labor of volunteers. As you hike these trails, please notice the work and craft that has been invested in maintaining them: clearing blowdowns, placing stone steps, building and clearing water bars to improve drainage and reduce erosion, clipping back brush, and refreshing blazes and signs. Hiking trails are human constructs, not natural ones, and even as you enjoy the natural vistas and wild places that these trails traverse, bear in mind that the trails themselves are a gift, passed from each generation of hikers to the next. Please pass it on!

Best wishes for safe, rewarding, and unforgettable hiking,

Ben Rose
Executive Director
The Green Mountain Club

P.S. For more information about the Green Mountain Club and how to join, refer to page 27 or check out www.greenmountainclub.org. See you on the trail!

Introduction

For anyone wishing to explore some of Vermont's greatest treasures—the Green Mountains—this book offers hours and days of hiking enjoyment. As a guide through the mountains along a variety of Vermont's hiking trails, this book offers directions for easy walks, ambitious day hikes, and weekend backpacking trips. The editors selected popular and lesser-known trails; some are quite easy, whereas a few are very strenuous. All of these hikes offer crisp mountain air and beautiful wilderness scenery, most with breathtaking views of surrounding pastoral valleys and neighboring mountain ranges. You can hike along sparkling streams, over suspension bridges, across open summits, and through secluded gulches bordered by ferns. Choose the hikes that excite and appeal to you the most.

The editors who selected these trails hiked them and evaluated them thoroughly. Although we encourage enthusiastic exploration of Vermont's hiking trails, we also caution you to consider your health and conditioning, your experience in the woods, the weather, your equipment, and a variety of other factors before exploring Vermont's backcountry wilderness. Please read the advice and information in the following section carefully before beginning your journey. Be prepared and be informed, and then thoroughly enjoy a safe journey into the Green Mountains of Vermont.

How to Use This Guide

Organized geographically and by difficulty in three regions of the state—south, central, and north—these hikes offer you a variety of terrain and scenery that represents each region. The beginning of each hike lists the general location, approximate distance and hiking time, vertical rise, difficulty rating, and a map of the area. This information allows you to select a hike based on your experience and the time available for your outing.

Before beginning a hike, take time to carefully plan your route, equipment, and supplies. Allow adequate time for unpredictable weather changes, and remember to leave a copy of your itinerary with a friend. Each section in this book contains the following information to help you prepare for your hike:

Total distance means the total number of miles you can expect to hike on the trails described. Each hike description indicates clearly whether this distance refers to a loop, a return by the same route, or a one-way hike (with cars spotted at both ends of the trail).

Hiking time includes all time spent walking or climbing and some time for resting and enjoying the views. The time listed very likely won't match your own time exactly, but it can serve as a consistent yardstick; your hiking time will likely exceed or be exceeded by the same difference for most any hike in this book, unless your hiking conditioning changes. The "book time," provides a convenient measure of your hiking ability.

Allow extra time for meals and swimming or fishing in the streams and ponds en route (remember that you need a Vermont fishing license). Times assume a steady pace and allow for differences in terrain. If you follow any alternate or side trails not included in

The summit register on Harmon Hill

the total distance, remember to adjust your hiking time expectations accordingly.

Vertical rise shows the total amount of climbing along the route. Although vertical rise may occur all in one climb (the difference between the lowest and highest points on the route), it frequently occurs over several climbs. If descents appear between these climbs, then the vertical rise noted for the hike exceeds the difference between the lowest and highest points on the hike. Remember that substantial vertical rise can turn even a short hike into a real challenge.

Difficulty ratings include easy, moderate, and strenuous classifications—although a few hikes fall in between these categories. Easy hikes are accessible to almost everyone, including first-time hikers, families with children, or someone with limited hiking time and a wish to enjoy Vermont's beautiful scenery. Moderate hikes require a degree of stamina; some previous hiking experience is advisable. Strenuous hikes are challenging outings for experienced hikers in good physical condition.

Maps, listed at the beginning of each hike, show you the area for the hike and provide information to order more detailed maps if you wish. This book contains maps based on United States Geological Survey (USGS) or Green Mountain National Forest (GMNF) topographic sheets. Use the maps in this guidebook only for reference; they are not suitable for map and compass orientation. See the "Route Planning and Ordering Maps" section for more information about where and how to order maps. In Vermont, the compass points about 15 degrees west of true north.

Some of the hikes follow routes on or along the Long Trail (LT), the 272-mile "footpath in the wilderness" through Vermont. See the "Hiking Information Available from the Green Mountain Club" section for guidebooks and maps offered by the Green Mountain Club (GMC).

The maps in this book are intended only as general guides to the trails. Logging, development, and other wilderness disturbances often necessitate changes in trail locations, although the editors took care to ensure the accuracy of trail descriptions and maps at the time of publication.

Hiking Guidelines

Guidelines are just that. We can't tell you how to go hiking. We can tell you what we've learned through years of experience and mostly trial and error. It's always best to learn from someone else's mistakes, but we're all going to have learning experiences on the trail—that's part of the adventure!

Hiking season in the Green Mountains begins in late spring and continues through summer and early fall. Most of the trails are not blazed for winter use; snow cover makes trails difficult or impossible to follow. The popularity of snowshoeing in recent years, however, has encouraged more and more winter use, and some trails offer the potential for enjoying the winter experience for appropriately experienced and equipped hikers. The GMC can provide suggestions for winter hikes. The "Winter Use" section contains additional information.

Mud Seasons

Vermonters joke that spring never comes to Vermont—winter leads directly into "mud season"! When warmth does come to the valleys, trails in higher elevations become wet and muddy. Hiking during "mud season"—from late March through late May—can damage the trails. Please wait until the trails are completely dry before hiking. During mud season:

- Turn back and select another hike if mud forces you to walk on the side of the tread way.
- Plan hikes in the hardwood forest at lower elevations.
- Avoid the spruce-fir (conifer) forests at higher elevations.
- Remember that the state of Vermont closes trails in the Camel's Hump and Mount Mansfield areas from mid-April until Memorial Day weekend. In addition to these areas, avoid Stratton Mountain, the Coolidge Range (Killington to Pico Peaks), Lincoln Ridge (Lincoln Gap to Appalachian Gap), and Jay Peak during mud season.

Similar muddy conditions appear in late fall, usually from late October until the snowpack forms. Although early snows leave moisture, the cover cannot protect the ground from damage. The freeze/thaw cycle, combined with overuse during this period, can make trails virtually impassable. Severe winter thaws can create similar conditions. During these times, hikers should find other recreational activities and allow the trails to freeze up or dry out. Such consideration protects the trails from further damage.

If you want to protect and preserve the trails, at all other times of the year walk *through* mud puddles, rather than around them, to minimize damage from "trail spread."

Temperatures

Average monthly Vermont temperature in June, July, and August reaches 60 degrees Fahrenheit (16 degrees Celsius) or higher; in September, 50 degrees (10 degrees C) or higher; in October, around 40 degrees (4 degrees C); and in early November, around 35 degrees (2 degrees C). At any time of the year, however, temperatures can drop below freezing.

Wildlife

Insects can make hiking difficult throughout the late spring and summer. Blackfly season usually lasts from mid-May until mid-June, although blackflies can appear throughout the summer in certain locations. Mosquitoes are a summer nuisance at dusk and dawn, especially in wet or swampy areas. Insect repellent, long-sleeve shirts, pants, and mosquito netting help minimize the effects of these pesky critters, so plan accordingly.

DEET, an effective ingredient in most insect repellents, can create health problems, particularly in children. If you choose to use a DEET-based product, apply it only to clothing and avoid using it on children. Or, use alternative repellents without DEE.T.

Mice, raccoons, squirrels, porcupines, bears, and deer occupy the forest all year round, and hikers usually see them at a distance if at all. Food attracts these animals, particularly at shelter sites. Mice often explore shelters at night; they can chew through a pack looking for food. Hang food and toiletries away from the sleeping area at night, and never offer a wild animal food.

Porcupines often chew wooden shelters and privies. Close and latch all doors where possible to keep them out. Also, hang boots at night because porcupines consider the salt in the linings a great delicacy.

Hanging food, maintaining a neat campsite, and carrying out waste and trash keeps animals at a distance. Never feed a wild animal, and avoid any animal that acts too tame, unafraid, or aggressive. They may have rabies. For this reason, do not touch any dead animal. If a wild animal bites you, wash the wound thoroughly with soap and water and get medical help quickly. Prompt medical treatment can successfully combat a rabies infection.

Winter Use

Hiking takes on a new aura in winter, with clear skies, no bugs, views unimpeded by leaves, and a quiet mountain solitude. Most hiking trails in Vermont are not designed for winter use. Snow usually covers blazes made 4 or 5 feet from the ground; snow-laden branches may block the way. Winter hikers need to anticipate Vermont's unpredictable and ever-changing weather conditions. Deep snow, short days, and the need to carry extra warm clothing and equipment pose practical problems, exacerbated by the winter hiker's need to break trail, a strenuous and exhausting process. Severe wind and weather conditions at higher elevations may make travel difficult or impossible.

Winter conditions extend from November to May in the Green Mountains, and the snowpack lingers until early June at higher elevations below tree line. Maximum snow depth in a typical year occurs in March.

By using snowshoes or skis for backcountry travel, you avoid making knee-deep holes in the snow (post-holing) and keep the trail open and accessible for those coming after you. At higher, windswept elevations, you may need crampons. Sanitation in the winter also poses a challenge. Carry a shovel and dig out the privy whenever possible. Use the privy instead of the snow in front of a shelter. No caretaker likes to arrive after the snowmelt to find piles of human waste left by winter hikers.

The GMC's Education Program offers winter hiking workshops. Today it's possible to walk into a gear store and buy all the equipment you need for a winter trek. You cannot buy experience! We highly recommend you take the time to learn from others the fundamentals of winter travel and safety. Many GMC sections and other outdoor organizations offer trips that help you gain experience with winter equipment and methods of travel. The Catamount Trail, for example, a winter trail that extends the length of Vermont, offers backcountry opportunities with cross-country ski resort facilities. For information and a guidebook, contact the Catamount Trail Association (802-864-5794).

Safety

The elements of safety include an awareness of weather conditions; packing sufficient clothing, food, and safety gear; carrying or obtaining water; maintaining "situational awareness," including proper route planning and following the blazed trails; and remaining aware of potential hazards along the route.

Weather

Expect unpredictable weather in Vermont, including the possibility of high-elevation snowstorms, even in summer! Rain and fog are common, and dangerous storms can appear suddenly. Check a weather report before starting to hike. If stormy weather threatens, either cancel the hike or select a hike at a lower elevation.

Clothing and Safety Gear

Anticipate wet weather by bringing adequate rain gear, a wool sweater, and a hat. Learn how to use a compass and always carry it—even on short hikes. Keep a first-aid kit and a supply of prepared, high-energy foods, such as nuts and dried fruits, in your pack at all times. The section "Clothing and Equipment" contains more information about what to wear on your hike.

Water

Water may look pure in the mountains, but it may carry an intestinal parasite called *Giardia lamblia,* even in pristine mountain environments. To prevent giardiasis (an un-pleasant infection that often causes cramps, diarrhea, nausea, and vomiting), you should chemically treat, boil, or filter water before drinking it. A 10-minute period of chemical treatment or boiling generally kills all viruses and bacteria. For the majority of hikes in this book, simply carry water with you—and remember to drink water at every rest stop, whether you feel thirsty or not. Everyone requires different amounts of water (usually between two and four quarts per day), depending on the weather condi-tions and how strenuous the hike.

"Situational Awareness"

Most trails listed in this book offer parking areas at trailheads. When parking your car, avoid obstructing traffic or blocking access to homes, farms, or woodlots.

Unfortunately, vandalism occurs at trail-heads; either remove all valuables from your car or lock them in your trunk. Remove your stereo if possible. Don't leave a note advis-ing friends of your plans. Empty the glove compartment and leave it open (unplug the light first!). Park in the open and parallel to the highway or head-in to the parking spaoo, if possible If you plan to stay overnight, you might consider leaving the car at a public spot such as a police or service station, or a ski area. Ask permission first; they may ask for a small parking fee. Then you can walk or get a ride to the trailhead.

Leave your itinerary with a friend, stay on your planned route, and sign in at all regis-ters. In case of a missing hiker, vandalism, or any other emergency, contact the Vermont State Police at the local number posted at most trailheads, the State Police Montpelier Dispatch Center (802-244-8727), or dial 911. After notifying the State Police, contact the GMC (802-244-7037).

Most trails in this book are blazed with either white or blue paint. Arrows and dou-ble blazes (one blaze over the other) indi-cate important turns and intersections. In open areas, or on higher elevations, blazes often appear on rocks; or cairns (a mound of rocks) and scree walls may mark the trail. As you hike, always look for the next blaze ahead of you. If you do not see a blaze after five minutes (approximately one-quarter mile), stop, look, and backtrack to make sure you are still on the trail. When unsure of the trail location, stop walking, avoid straying farther, and calmly evaluate your sit-uation. Remain in one place, check your map, blow your whistle (three blasts), and stay warm until someone finds you.

Hypothermia

The deadly and dangerous condition of hy-pothermia begins with the cooling of the body's core temperature, usually from heat loss and the inability to maintain a constant internal temperature. This condition can occur at any time, not necessarily in winter's below-zero temperatures. Instead, "hy-pothermia weather" often occurs on rainy, windy days with temperatures 60 degrees F (16 degrees C) or below.

The symptoms of hypothermia include poor judgment, forgetfulness, and confu-sion. Victims may lack motor control and be-come unable to perform simple tasks, such as buttoning a jacket. Their gait becomes unsteady, and they may slur their speech. Other signs of hypothermia include the in-ability to keep fingers and toes warm, un-controllable shivering, or extreme and unexpected fatigue. Extreme hypothermia can result in lethargy, coma, and death.

Prevention can help avoid hypothermia. Keep the head covered to minimize loss of body heat through radiational cooling. Avoid sitting on frozen ground. During breaks, sit on a pack or foam pad. Wear a windbreaker

Descending from the summit of Mount Mansfield

to prevent the wind from cooling the body, and cover up to minimize the cooling effects of perspiration.

Carry snacks and water while hiking, and eat and drink frequently. Bring extra food in case of emergency. Dress in layers to wick perspiration away from the body—and shed layers when you get warm. Wear wool or synthetic materials (such as polypropylene), or carry them in your pack on hot days.

A steady hiking pace helps minimize perspiration, which can dampen clothing and cool the body. Rest briefly, and resume hiking before your body cools too much. If you anticipate extreme conditions, consider carrying a tarp to create an emergency shelter; bring matches and a stove so you can make hot drinks to help maintain the body's core temperature.

Early detection of hypothermia simplifies treatment. With victims who continue to walk and talk, simply get them out of the wind and allow them to change into dry clothing. Cover their heads, provide something to eat and drink, and continue moving.

If the victim does not warm up after these simple actions, ask a healthy companion to prewarm a sleeping bag, and then place both individuals in the bag. Or place bottles of warm water around the victim's neck, armpits, and groin and wrap them in the sleeping bag. Evacuate the victim as soon as their condition improves. In rare cases, a victim falls unconscious. Such an emergency means you must handle them gently and evacuate them quickly.

Lightning

Although a rare occurrence, lightning does strike hikers every year. Avoid hiking when weather reports predict thunderstorms; find shelter immediately if you are caught in a storm. Stay away from summits, ridgelines, and open clearings. If the storm arises suddenly and you find yourself on a ridgeline, move quickly downhill if possible, or seek

---

the middle of the ridge and avoid the shoulder at each end. Crouch down, or roll into a ball, preferably on your pack or other insulating object. Avoid contact with the ground. Spread out so that a single bolt cannot strike every member of the group.

In a forest, take shelter in a stand of smaller trees. Avoid moist areas, such as wet gullies and crevices and small depressions where ground currents may travel. Stay out of small caves. Tents offer no protection from lightning. Avoid tall structures, such as television towers, flag poles, tall trees, or hilltops.

If lightning does strike, the victim may experience burns, bruising, unconsciousness, or cardiac arrest. Call 911 if possible. Someone may need to perform artificial respiration and CPR until help arrives. Maintain breathing for the victim even if he or she appears lifeless; victims recover quickly once they gain the ability to breathe for themselves.

Hunting

Hunting, like hiking, is a traditional use of Vermont's woods. Hikers and hunters share the forests of Vermont during the fall, usually from September through December. Deer season mostly occurs in November and wild turkey season in May. Wear bright visible clothing during hunting season, preferably fluorescent orange. Avoid brown, tan, black, or patches of white that might be mistaken for the white tail of a deer. The Vermont Department of Fish and Wildlife (802-241-3700) can provide more information about hunting season and safe practices.

Clothing and Equipment

The most important rule for clothing, even in summer, is to dress in layers or bring extra clothing with you. The shirt that feels cool with perspiration on a hot summer day may chill you to the bone on a windy and cold mountain summit. Always bring an extra layer of clothing for protection.

No list is perfect, but lists become essential to eliminate the possibility of leaving the camera behind....

Boots–Because most of the trails in this book are primitive footpaths, not specially surfaced trails, boots offer the best support and traction. On the other hand, lug soles are culprits in the ongoing debate over trail erosion. Beginners should wear sturdy and comfortable boots; experienced hikers used to hiking on rough terrain might consider wearing shoes with more trail-friendly soles. Some of us hike in sandals....

Socks–Good socks are almost more important than good shoes! Bring an extra pair of socks in case your feet get wet.

Wind jacket/rain gear/breathable shell– Remember, Vermont's unpredictable weather–always be prepared with rain gear! In warm weather, an umbrella might be more comfortable than a rain jacket. Ponchos and umbrellas are disasters in windy weather.

Sweater or jacket–Warm, dry clothing offers comfort and protection against winds and cooler temperatures at higher elevations. Wool is still the fiber of choice. A wool shirt wears like iron and doesn't melt near campfires or flaring camp stoves.

Hat–You can lose 40 percent of body heat through an uncovered head; headgear keeps you warm.

Day pack–The standard rule of thumb here is whatever size pack you have, you will fill it. It is important to get a pack large enough to carry what you need for a comfortable hike, but bigger is not necessarily better.

Guidebook, maps, and compass–Learn how to use a compass. You may almost never need it, but when you do, you really need it. The GMC Education Program offers map and compass courses regularly.

Water bottle(s) or *canteen(s)*—Proper hydration minimizes injuries and fatigue while ensuring your general well-being.

First-aid kit—Include moleskin or similar products for blisters, Band-Aids in assorted sizes, triangular bandage or bandanna, adhesive tape, antiseptic cream, gauze. Pack everything in a waterproof, sealable plastic bag.

Trail lunch—Food provides the fuel for your hike. Bring a sandwich, fruit, and snacks for the day, and extra high-energy food (energy bars, dried fruit, nuts) for emergencies. Here we recommend carrying food you usually eat. A hike is the wrong time to change your diet. Hikers do march on their stomachs.

Flashlight (or headlamp)—with working batteries, a spare set of batteries, and a spare bulb. Worth checking before each hike—again, when you need it, you really need it.

Matches and/or lighter—Bring waterproof matches or seal everything in a plastic bag.

Toilet paper and trowel
Pocketknife
Whistle—Three short blasts indicate an emergency and help rescuers locate you.
Insect repellent
Sunscreen
Sunglasses (optional)
Camera and binoculars (optional)

Additional items required for backpacking trips:

Frame pack (internal or external)—again, get a pack big enough for the gear you need. That 6,000-cubic-inch pack may look great, but you might not want to carry that much gear up the mountain.

Tent or tarp

Sleeping bag and pad—Carry in a waterproof sack. A garbage bag inside that is good insurance. Remember that temperature ratings, like hiking times, vary for individuals. If you sleep cold, get a warmer sleeping bag.

Backpacking stove and spare fuel
Cooking gear and eating utensils
Additional food
Extra clothing—Place in a waterproof sack.
Litter bags—Pack out all trash!

Leave No Trace™

LEAVE NO TRACE™ is a nationwide effort to educate backcountry travelers about the importance of practicing low-impact camping and travel techniques to minimize the potential negative impacts we can have on the land, wildlife, and other visitors. "Minimum impact" and "leave no trace" are concepts far more involved than simply giving a hoot and not polluting. Extensive scientific research has revealed widespread damage caused by "loving to death" the favorite places we visit and recreate in. The **LEAVE NO TRACE™** program with its seven principles (listed below) is part of the solution to promoting sustainable use of the backcountry. The GMC offers a variety of education workshops teaching these principles for travelers to understand the ethics and practice the outdoor skills. We encourage you to contact us and find out more about the courses at 802-244-7037 or groups @greenmountainclub.org. Or visit our web site: www.greenmountainclub.org. The seven principles are as follows:

Plan Ahead and Prepare. Familiarize yourself with local regulations. Visit in small groups; split larger parties into groups of four to eight. Groups should plan to not occupy shelters. Repackage food to minimize waste. Prepare adequately for extreme weather, hazards, and emergencies. Trails can be difficult and travel slower than it appears on a map, *especially in northern Vermont*. Purify *all* drinking water. Carry and know how to use a map and compass. Bring enough tents for everyone.

Travel and Camp on Durable Surfaces. Stay on the trail; avoid shortcuts that erode soil and damage vegetation. Camp in designated sites. Use tent platforms if available to avoid compacting soil. Concentrate activities on existing trails and campsites. Avoid camping where impact is just beginning. Walk single file in the middle of the trail, even when wet or muddy, to avoid widening the tread way. Walk on rocks whenever possible, especially in fragile areas such as shorelines and alpine zones.

Dispose of Waste Properly. If you pack it in, pack it out! Shelters and campsites are equipped with privies. Otherwise, bury human and pet waste in 6- to 8-inch cat holes at least 200 feet away from water sources. Pack out all trash, including hygiene products (opaque bags are helpful). To wash yourself or your dishes, carry water 200 feet away from streams or ponds and use little or no soap. Strain food particles from dishwater and pack out; scatter the dishwater. Keep pets away from water sources to protect water quality.

Leave What You Find. Take only pictures; leave only footprints. Flowers and other naturally occurring objects are best enjoyed in their natural states. Removal of these items is *illegal* on state and federal lands. Altering a campsite is not necessary. Let others enjoy nature and cultural artifacts as you originally found them. Please don't carve into trees or shelters along the trail. After breaking down camp, leave your site cleaner than you found it.

Minimize Campfire Impact. Know local regulations; wood fires may be prohibited. Campfires cause lasting impacts to the backcountry and are discouraged. Use a portable stove for cooking instead of a fire. Where permitted, if you choose to build a fire, use only preexisting fire rings. Keep fires small using only dead, downed wood. To minimize impacts to the campsite, collect wood on the way in. Burn all wood and coals to ash, extinguish completely, then scatter cool ashes.

Respect Wildlife. Bring binoculars and observe wildlife from a distance. Feeding animals damages their health, alters natural behaviors, and exposes them to predators; *do not feed.* Protect wildlife and your food by storing food securely. If you must bring a pet, keep it leashed and dispose of its waste properly (see above), especially in fragile areas and at campsites. Consider leaving your pet at home.

Be Considerate of Other Visitors. Respect other trail users and protect the quality of their experience. Keep your group size small; no more than 10 on overnighters or trips to fragile areas (alpine summits, pond sites and shorelines, and designated wilderness areas) and no more than 20 on day trips. Be courteous and yield to others on the trail. Take breaks away from the trail and other visitors on durable surfaces. Travel and camp quietly. Let nature's sounds prevail by avoiding loud voices and noises.

For further information about **LEAVE NO TRACE™**, visit www.LNT.org , or join a GMC workshop.

Site and Summit Caretakers

From early May to early November, GMC caretakers are stationed at several sensitive, high-use overnight sites and several alpine areas along the LT. Their informal conversation serves to educate hikers about leave-no-trace practices; they also help maintain trails and shelters. At overnight sites, they manage sewage through composting. As summit caretakers, they discuss the fragile alpine ecosystems, enforce camping and fire regulations, and offer first aid and assistance.

As experienced hikers themselves, caretakers can make suggestions and offer basic information about hiking, natural history, and the GMC.

Trail Courtesy

Please respect all trail lands. Some trails cross private land; others follow public property. Leave no trace. Carry out all trash. Remember that landowners use the lands adjacent to the trail for farming, grazing, maple sugaring, or logging, all vital to Vermont's economy and way of life.

Private Property—Many of the trails in this guide are located on private property. Please be considerate and appreciative of these landowners, and treat their property with respect to ensure that trails on private property remain open. Do not block traffic or access to private homes when parking at trailheads, and always check with landowners before parking on private property.

Pets—Although your dog may be your best friend, consider leaving it at home. It is often difficult to prevent dogs from contaminating water supplies; they frequently create problems with wildlife, especially porcupines; some hikers or children are afraid of even friendly pets; and dogs may hurt themselves on some of the rougher portions of the trail. If you choose to bring a well-trained dog with you, leash it around tent sites, shelters, water sources, and in the alpine zone. Carry a water bowl so it won't have to drink from water sources, bring extra water for your pet on warm days, and pack biscuits and/or kibble to sustain

your pet on longer, more strenuous hikes. Examine your pet's feet for torn pads, bleeding, or sores (pet stores offer "booties" to protect paws from rocks and abrasions). Bury pet waste as you would human waste.

This does seem to be an intimidating list of do's and don'ts; they will quickly become second nature and will ensure an enjoyable hike with your pet and minimize friction with other hikers. We do recommend bringing pliers if you hike with your pet—porcupines are not as common as they used to be, but most every hiking dog will get quilled eventually; being prepared will minimize this trail emergency. And experience has shown that dogs don't learn from this trauma; some of us have had to carry out severely quilled dogs for a veterinarian's attention.

Trash and Waste—The GMC firmly believes in one trail motto: "Pack it in, pack it out." Avoid leaving litter on the trail or in the woods, and pick up litter when someone ignores this rule. Because human waste can damage water quality, use privies when available or bury human (and animal) waste, including toilet paper, 4 to 6 inches deep and at least 200 feet from any trail or water supply.

Group Use

Organized groups—such as school groups, camps, and scouts—can use these hikes to plan their next outing. With experienced leadership, a good leader-to-participant ratio (usually one to four), and a manageable size, each individual in the group can enjoy a successful hike.

GMC promotes a group-use policy that limits group size (including leaders) to 10 individuals for overnights and 20 for day hikes. When possible, the GMC recommends smaller group sizes (4 to 6 for overnights and 10 for day hikes) so that leaders can provide each participant with maximum attention and security and the group does not strain existing backcountry resources at shelter and camping sites. At certain shelters, signs encourage groups to use designated tenting areas and avoid shelters entirely. Groups should bring sufficient equipment to tent when shelters are full. Any hiker, and especially those in groups, should accommodate new arrivals and make space for them in shelters or tenting areas.

To minimize impact, some groups break into smaller units and leave at half-hour intervals, and resist the temptation to reconvene until they've returned to the trailhead. Others use different trails to reach a summit or scenic view. Still others hike in opposite directions on the same trail and trade car keys at a middle point. When possible, consider breaking up the group with several experienced leaders and hike in different areas.

GMC staff members can provide planning help and recommendations for group use and suitable hiking areas.

Trail Work

Many trails in Vermont's beautiful mountains include some man-made modifications, which help preserve the tread way and make for drier hiking boots. The Civilian Conservation Corps (CCC), a government work program begun during the Great Depression of the 1930s, completed some of this work. The Long Trail Patrol and GMC volunteers continue the task of trail construction and maintenance today. This book refers to the following trail construction terms:

Puncheon–Small wooden bridges on one or more log or board planks held off the ground on sills.

Turnpiking–A raised trail bed formed by placing logs on either side of the trail and filling between them with dirt and gravel.

Water Bars–A drainage system of log or rock construction that provides the best defense against trail erosion. Water bars include three parts: the bar, built of log or rock; the apron, a shallow slope to funnel water to the bar; and the ditch, which carries water from the bar and off the trail.

Camping and Fires

Camping and fires are restricted on most Vermont lands, depending on whether the land is private, state, or federal. Contact the Green Mountain National Forest; Vermont Department of Forests, Parks and Recreation; or the GMC for more information. Most backpackers carry a portable gas- or alcohol-fueled stove for cooking.

Peregrine Falcons

The following trails in this book pass by the nesting sites of peregrine falcons: Mount Horrid's Great Cliff (hike 19), Rattlesnake Point (hike 23), Mount Pisgah (hike 42), and Sterling Pond and Elephant's Head (hike 47).

The use of the pesticide DDT after World War II almost eliminated these beautiful birds. After the government banned the use of DDT in 1972, the Peregrine Fund at Cornell University and the United States Fish and Wildlife Service started a reintroduction program that released captive-born young falcons on many cliff sites. The Vermont Institute of Natural Science, the Vermont Department of Fish and Wildlife, and the U.S. Forest Service sponsored the peregrine release–or "hacking"–program in Vermont. The first wild nesting pair returned to Vermont at Mount Pisgah in 1985.

Although delisted from the Federal Endangered Species List in 1999, the U.S. Fish and Wildlife Service continues to monitor peregrine falcon populations. The

Vermont Endangered Species Law still lists the peregrine falcon as endangered, which ensures protection at the state level.

Governmental agencies monitor most peregrine nesting sites in Vermont every year. In Smugglers' Notch, for example, monitoring begins early in the season (around April) to determine nesting sites; the birds historically use several different nesting sites on both sides of the notch. Nesting season usually runs from February through July.

Humans can disturb nesting peregrine falcons and force them to abandon their nests if approached. To protect these birds, the state temporarily closes trails that come close to the nest site or bring hikers onto exposed areas above the nest. Because nesting sites vary year to year, the Vermont Forest, Parks, and Recreation Department works with the Vermont Fish and Wildlife Department to minimize both disturbance to the birds and the loss of recreational opportunities.

Watch these majestic raptors only from a distance, using either powerful binoculars or a telescope. Please obey any posted signs, and do not disturb the birds. For more information, contact the GMC or the Department of Fish and Wildlife at 802-241-3700.

Arctic-Alpine Vegetation

Several of the higher summits in this guidebook feature unique ecosystems with fragile arctic-alpine plant communities. This rare and beautiful plant life remains from an era when ice sheets covered northern New England.

When the most recent glaciers from the Laurentian Ice Sheet retreated between 8,000 and 12,000 years ago, arctic plants grew in exposed areas. As the climate warmed, most of these plants retreated north—except for those on a few mountaintops where the climate resembles the Arctic regions 1,000 miles to the north of Vermont. Shallow soils, high winds, low temperatures, a short growing season, high precipitation (100 or more inches a year), and heavy fog (the alpine plants absorb 5 to 30 inches of fog moisture each year in addition to precipitation) allow only a few species to survive. Those that remain grow very slowly. For example, it takes approximately eighty years for a tree near the timberline to grow 2 inches in diameter.

The survival of this rare vegetation, much of which looks like ordinary grass, is precarious. The same shallow soil and vigorous climatic conditions that allow it to grow make the environment especially vulnerable to hiker disturbances. When a small portion of alpine tundra is destroyed, the wind rapidly scours large holes in the damaged turf, and the soil quickly erodes. Removal of rocks from the grassy tundra is especially harmful in this respect. Fires destroy not only the ground cover plants, but also the thin underlying layer of humus. Because excessive trampling of plants and soil leads to further loss of rare vegetation, please stay on the marked trails and rock outcrops.

The Green Mountain Club

Since its founding, the GMC's primary purpose has been to build, maintain, and protect hiking trails and shelters for the enjoyment of Vermont's residents and visitors.

In 1910, the GMC founded the Long Trail (LT), the nation's oldest long-distance hiking trail. Completed in 1930, the 272-mile LT follows the ridgeline of the Green Mountains from Massachusetts to Canada and encompasses more than 175 miles of side trails and nearly 70 rustic cabins and lean-to shelters. The entire 445-mile Long Trail System is managed and maintained by GMC field staff and hundreds of dedicated volunteers in cooperation with private landowners and state and federal agencies. The LT provided the inspiration for the founders of the Appalachian Trail. Today, the two trails share 104 miles of the present route.

In 1985, the GMC learned that 34 of the 65 miles of the LT on private land in northern Vermont were for sale. Rising real estate values, the unsettled economics of the forest products industry, and rapid development in Vermont created a volatile land market. The GMC also faced serious problems with landowners who wanted the LT removed from their property or who wanted to use the land for purposes incompatible with the trail.

Convinced of the need to save the scenic quality, environment, wildlife habitat, and continuity of the LT, the GMC started the Long Trail Protection Campaign and achieved important results. The fund has raised more than $8 million and permanently protected over 55 miles of the LT in northern Vermont, 14 miles of side trails, and 22,315 acres of backcountry land.

The effort to save the LT continues. Vermont is experiencing a construction and population boom as well as tremendous pressures on land use. About eight miles of the LT and 5 miles of side trails are still in need of protection. The GMC continues the effort to preserve these high mountain lands that are so important to Vermonters and the thousands of people who visit the state each year.

Membership

Anyone interested in hiking and in Vermont's mountains can join the GMC. Membership in the GMC helps protect and preserve the Long Trail System; annual dues support trail maintenance, education, publications, and trail protection activities.

Anyone who wishes to participate in local outdoor and trail activities may join the GMC as a *section* or *at-large* member. Each section (chapter) schedules four-season activities including hikes, potluck dinners, bike trips, cross-country skiing/snowshoeing, and canoeing/kayaking. Section members maintain portions of the LT and its shelters and receive a section-oriented newsletter listing upcoming events. *At-large membership* lets you support the GMC without joining a section.

Both section and at-large members receive a subscription to the GMC's quarterly periodical, *The Long Trail News,* which provides up-to-date information on trail and shelter conditions, hiking, statewide trails, club history, and a club activity calendar. All members receive discounts on club publications (such as maps and guidebooks), items carried in the GMC bookstore, and opportunities to participate in wide-ranging club activities.

Today's 14 sections include Bennington, Brattleboro, Bread Loaf (Middlebury), Burlington, Connecticut, Killington (Rutland), Laraway (St. Albans), Manchester, Montpelier, Northeast Kingdom, Northern Frontier (Montgomery), Ottauquechee (Woodstock), Sterling (Stowe-Morrisville-Johnson), and Worcester (Massachusetts).

The GMC welcomes volunteers and provides many opportunities for involvement with the club's activities. No experience is necessary, and newcomers are always welcome. The club sponsors education workshops year-round for folks looking for additional information, new perspectives, or just a great day in the woods.

If you would like more information about the GMC, the trails in this book, other hiking opportunities in Vermont, volunteer activities, or membership, please contact us. We will happily help you plan your next hiking adventure.

The Green Mountain Club
4711 Waterbury-Stowe Road
Waterbury Center, VT 05677
802-244-7037
www.greenmountainclub.org

You can visit the GMC in Waterbury, Vermont. From I-89 in Waterbury (exit 10), follow VT 100 north 4 miles. The headquarters are located in the red barn and office building on the left (west) side of VT 100. Alternatively, from the intersection of VT 108 and VT 100 in Stowe, follow VT 100 south 6 miles to the headquarters buildings.

The Marvin B. Gameroff Hiker Center houses the club's information services, educational displays, bookstore, and field programs. The center provides information about backcountry recreational opportunities throughout Vermont. During the winter, the club hosts the James P. Taylor winter slide show and lecture series, which highlights outdoor recreation adventures. Business hours are Monday through Friday from 9:00 A.M. to 5:00 P.M. year-round. From Memorial Day to Columbus Day, the hiker center remains open seven days a week from 9:00 A.M. to 5:00 P.M.

Hiking Information Available from the Green Mountain Club

The GMC issues a variety of publications about hiking and backpacking in Vermont and welcomes inquiries about trail conditions and planning. To order GMC publications, see the order form in the back of this book.

Guidebooks and Maps

Long Trail Guide (25th Edition 2003)—The latest edition contains 17 color topographical maps, with complete descriptions of the LT, its side trails and shelters, and the Appalachian Trail in Vermont; suggested hikes, helpful hints, and winter-use suggestions.

Day Hiker's Guide to Vermont (4th Edition 2002)—Companion volume to the *Long Trail Guide*. Comprehensive coverage of more than 200 short hikes throughout the state; 12 color topographical maps and 34 black-and-white maps; hiking tips and suggestions.

Long Trail End-to-Ender's Guide—A must-have guide for long-distance LT hikers. Annually updated, this supplement to the *Long Trail Guide* provides detailed information about trail conditions, overnight accommodations, trail towns, mail drops, and transportation.

Mount Mansfield Booklet

The Tundra Walk—An Interpretive Guide to the Mount Mansfield Alpine Region (2002)—This illustrated brochure describes a 0.5-mile natural-history hike along the LT on the summit ridgeline of Mount Mansfield.

Green Mountain Club History

Green Mountain Adventure, Vermont's Long Trail (1st Edition 1985, Second Printing 1989)—An illustrated history of the GMC by Jane Curtis, Will Curtis, and Frank Lieberman. Ninety-six pages of rare black-and-white photographs and anecdotes of the GMC's first 75 years.

Pamphlets

The Long Trail: A Footpath in the Wilderness—Brochure with information and suggestions on hiking the LT. Free with legal-sized self-addressed stamped envelope.

Route Planning and Ordering Maps

The USGS provides mapping services for the United States. Most hikers use the 1:24,000-scale (or 7.5-minute) topographic (or *topo*) maps, although smaller-scale maps are available. Many Vermont topo maps date from the late 1980s, so they may not include all details, such as home or business construction sites. These maps provide topographic details, such as elevations, drainages, and other natural landmarks. USGS also provides downloadable maps from its web sites.

Use the following address information to obtain maps from the USGS and its online retailers:

United States Geological Survey
Branch of Information Services
Box 25286, Denver Federal Center
Denver, CO 80225
303-202-4700

Most sources of USGS maps can send you free grids for 7.5-minute topo map quadrants for any state. Order maps from the grid by quadrant. Before ordering, make sure you know the quadrangle (or quad) where you plan to hike (for example, USGS 7.5' Bolton). USGS defines each quadrangle map by a nearby town or natural feature.

The USGS lists retail vendors across the country who stock government maps. Most offer USGS quads for all states. Many vendors operate on a prepaid basis only. They accept phone orders and forward the maps after receiving your payment.

Your local sporting goods shop or bookstore may also carry USGS maps. Check the phone directory under "Maps–Dealers." The USGS web site lists Vermont area map vendors at: http://rockyweb.cr.usgs.gov/public/acis/map-dealers/vt.html.

In addition, you may order GMNF maps from the:

Forest Supervisor's Headquarters
Green Mountain National Forest
231 North Main Street
Rutland, VT 05701
802-747-6700 or 747-6765

GMNF maps only include those quadrangles in which the forest is located. Send a prepaid order to receive these maps.

Other Resources

For additional information on hiking in Vermont, you may wish to contact one or more of the following organizations.

On Federal Lands

Green Mountain National Forest
Supervisor's Office
231 North Main Street, Route 7
Rutland, VT 05701
802-747-6700
http://www.fs.fed.us/r9/gmfl/

On State Lands

Department of Forest, Parks, and Recreation
Agency of Natural Resources
103 South Main Street
Waterbury, VT 05671-0601
802-241-3655
http://www.anr.state.vt.us/

On the Appalachian Trail *(AT Guide to New Hampshire and Vermont)*

Appalachian Trail Conference
799 Washington Street
P.O. Box 807
Harpers Ferry, WV 25425
304-535-6331
http://www.atconf.org/

Winter Hiking and Snowshoeing

The following books contain information about winter hiking and snowshoeing in Vermont:

The Catamount Trail Guidebook (Seventh Edition, August 1999), a guide to the 300-mile backcountry ski trail that runs the length of Vermont. Published by the Catamount Trail Association and available from GMC.

Winter Trails Vermont & New Hampshire: The Best Cross-Country Ski and Snowshoe Trails, by Marty Basch (Globe Pequot Press, 2001).

Recommended References

A highly subjective list of references includes:

The Complete Walker IV, by Colin Fletcher and Chip Rawlins, 2002; Alfred A. Knopf; an exhaustive and thorough look at hiking gear with time-tested opinions and philosophies.

Winterwise, by John Dunn, 1996; Adirondack Mountain Club; a great guide to enjoying the great white north safely.

Be Expert with Map and Compass, by Bjorn Kjellstrom, 1994; IDG Books Worldwide; the guide for understanding map and compass, not only for staying found but for getting to where you want to go.

Backwoods Ethics, by Laura and Guy Waterman, 1993; Countryman Press; a provocative discussion of the balance between management and freedom in the backcountry, well worth seeking out to better understand some of the issues and controversies associated with protecting and enjoying our recreational resources.

The Nature of Vermont, by Charles W. Johnson, 1998; University Press of New England; a great guide to Vermont's environment.

Leave No Trace, by Annette McGivney, 1998; The Mountaineers; a more detailed look at walking softly through the woods.

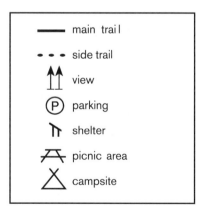

Bald Mountain Trail

JEFF NUGENT

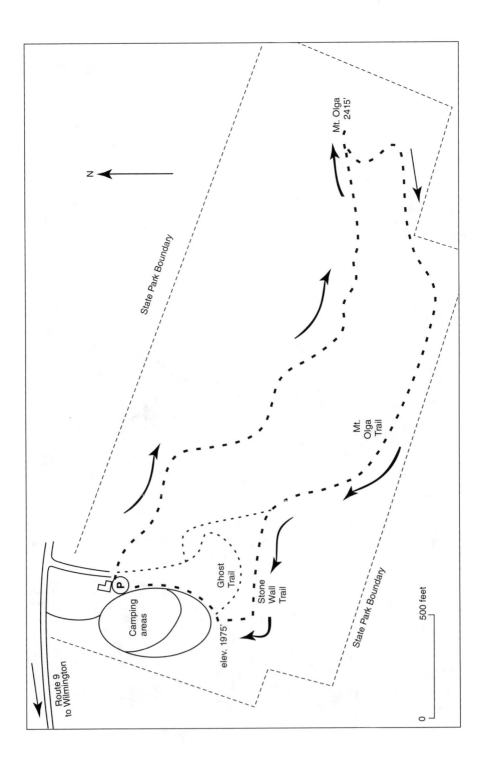

N

State Park Boundary

Mt. Olga
2415'

Mt.
Olga
Trail

Ghost
Trail

Stone
Wall
Trail

elev. 1975'

Camping
areas

P

Route 9
to Wilmington

State Park Boundary

0   500 feet

1

Mount Olga

Total distance: 1.6-mile loop

Hiking time: 1½ hours

Vertical rise: 500 feet

Rating: Easy to moderate

Map: USGS 7.5' Jacksonville

The trail up Mount Olga is located in Molly Stark State Park, which is named for the wife of General John Stark. During the Revolutionary War in 1777, the general sent Molly a message asking her to "Send every man from the farm that will come and let the haying go." Molly organized the farmers and, along with two hundred other men, went to the general's aid. After the Battle of Bennington, General Stark returned home with one of the six brass cannons captured from the British as a token of gratitude to Molly.

This park, one of the smaller ones in the state park system, is a beautiful place to picnic or camp. A day-use fee is charged during the summer months.

How to Get There

Molly Stark State Park is 3.4 miles east of Wilmington on VT 9. Ample parking is available.

The Trail

You may want to pick up the free park brochure "Hiking Trail to Mount Olga" before beginning your hike. The trail begins on the east side of the park road opposite the caretaker's home. A sign indicates a distance of 0.8 mile to the fire tower. Follow the blue-blazed trail down a short embankment on steps, across a small wooden bridge over a stream, and up a slight to moderate grade. The trail is covered with a soft carpet of needles. You soon cross over an old stone wall, turn sharply left, and continue your ascent through a forest of stately spruce. Pass

Looking west from Mount Olga

among boulders and ferns, and then cross the remains of another low stone wall.

Climb again on moderate grades until you reach a rough-barked red maple tree growing on the left side of the trail. This tree has four distinct large trunks that sprouted from a cut-over stump. The multiple maple stems support a small yellow birch tree. The trail narrows, becomes steeper, climbs up a few stone steps, and at 0.7 mile reaches a junction. From the junction, where an information board and map are located, bear left, and steeply ascend to the wooded summit (elevation 2,415 feet), which has a fire tower, three old buildings, a utility shed, and a radio relay tower.

The summit was established as a fire lookout, with a wooden tower, in the early 1930s. In 1949–50 the wooden tower was removed, and the steel tower from Bald Mountain in Townshend was transferred to Mount Olga. This tower, which is still standing, was abandoned as a fire lookout in the 1970s. Climb the fire tower for a beautiful 360-degree panoramic view of southern Vermont and northwestern Massachusetts.

Directly opposite the relay tower is Haystack Mountain, the only mountain with a significant peak. Mount Snow is to right of Haystack, at the end of the Deerfield Ridge. Stratton Mountain is the large mountain farther to the right. Looking to the left of Haystack, VT 9 leads to the village of Wilmington. The windmills of the Searsburg Wind Power Facility and Haystack Mountain (see hike 5) stand out on the horizon, and a portion of Harriman Reservoir is visible. Mount Greylock, the highest point in Massachusetts, can also be seen to the west.

Return to the trail junction, turn left onto the return loop, and descend on easy grades through numerous rock outcrops. Pass between giant boulders and ledges, and across a small bridge. The area beyond the boulders, in contrast to the evergreen forest through which you passed on your ascent of Mount Olga, is composed of maple, beech, birch, and ash; no conifers are in sight. Continue your gentle descent to a long, straight section of trail. Turn left, and parallel an old stone wall through overgrown, sometimes wet pastureland. The old stone wall and trail soon turn right and reach the campground road across from campsite 9. Turn right, and follow the road back to your car at 1.6 miles.

2

Prospect Rock (Manchester)

Total distance: 3 miles

Hiking time: 2½ hours

Vertical rise: 1,100 feet

Rating: Strenuous

Map: USGS 7.5' Manchester

This popular trail up Prospect Rock offers views of the Lye Brook Wilderness Area, Mount Equinox, and Manchester Center.

How to Get There

From US 7, take the Manchester exit #4 (0.0 mile) and follow VT 11 and 30 east for 0.5 mile to its junction with East Manchester Road on your right. Turn right onto East Manchester Road, and after about 150 feet, turn left onto Rootville Road. Follow it 0.5 mile to the concrete water tower on your right and a small gravel driveway and house. There is limited parking near the water tower at 1.05 miles, just before the NO PARKING signs. Do not block the road, and do not park near or drive past the signs.

The Trail

Begin your hike up Old Rootville Road to a Green Mountain National Forest signboard on your right. Continue on the moderately graded old road up the side of the mountain, and listen to the brook flowing on your right. The small brook comes into view on your right, and the old road ascends more steeply up the mountain.

This hike is wonderful in the fall because of the many different trees: white and yellow birch, maple, oak, and spruce. At 0.3 mile, the road crosses the brook and is soon met by another small brook on your right. Continue to crisscross the brook until you reach a spring box on your left, where the brook turns to the left away from the road. After climbing to another spring at 0.8 mile,

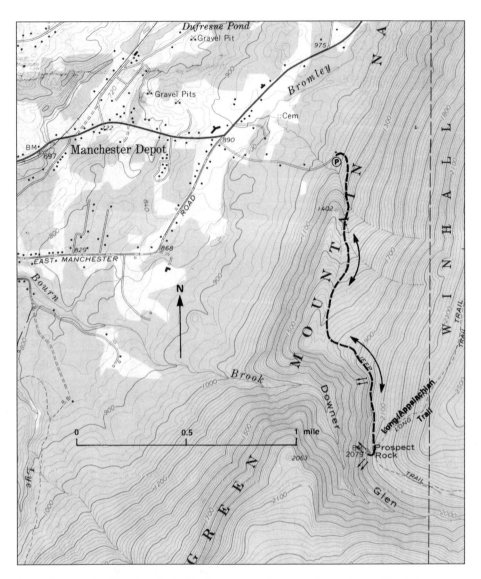

leave the sound of the brooks behind and enjoy a deep quiet interrupted only by birds and chipmunks.

The old road soon levels off and passes through a beautiful birch stand filled with sunlight—on days when clouds don't intercede. The trail eventually starts climbing again with a steep drop-off to your right and views of Downer Glen. At this point, the road is carved out of the side of the mountain and levels off before climbing on easier grades. Manchester Center and Mount Equinox can be seen through the trees.

At 1.5 miles, you reach a junction where the white-blazed Long Trail climbs the embankment off to your left and goes north to Spruce Peak and Bromley Mountain. Straight ahead, the Long Trail follows the

Enjoying the view from Prospect Rock

DAVE HARDY

road south to Stratton Pond. To the right, a spur leads about 200 feet west to Prospect Rock.

From the rock, high above Downer Glen, you can see the highway and Manchester Center. To the northwest, up the valley, is Dorset. Mount Aeolus is to the right of the valley, and Mount Equinox, the highest peak of the Taconic Range, can be seen to the left of the valley.

After enjoying the views, return along the same trails to your car.

3

White Rocks/Ice Beds Trail

Total distance: 2 miles

Hiking time: 1½ hours

Vertical rise: 460 feet

Rating: Easy

Map: USGS 7.5' Wallingford

This relatively easy hike offers wonderful views of the White Rocks Cliff and the "Ice Beds," where ice, formed beneath the rocks during the previous winter, chills a meltwater stream.

How to Get There

Drive east on VT 140 from its US 7 junction in Wallingford to Sugar Hill Road at 2.2 miles. Turn right, drive about 150 yards on Sugar Hill Road, and turn right onto U.S. Forest Service (USFS) Road 52. Continue to the White Rocks Picnic Area at 2.8 miles. The picnic area has ample parking for 30 cars, along with picnic facilities and outhouses. The picnic area is also the trailhead for a different trail—the Keewaydin Trail—leading 0.4 mile to the Long Trail.

The Trail

Near the entrance to the picnic area a trailhead sign marks the beginning of the blue-blazed Ice Beds Trail. You immediately pass through a small wet area on bridges and turnpiking. Large rock outcrops appear on your left, and boulders dot the area as you hike up the hillside. The trail swings to your right and climbs through boulders and softwoods. Hike along a switchback, then ascend more steeply to a trail junction at 0.3 mile.

From this point, the White Rocks Trail leads left to a spectacular view of the White Rocks Cliff and the Otter Creek Valley to the southwest. A talc mine in South Wallingford on US 7 is also visible.

Because peregrine falcons have returned

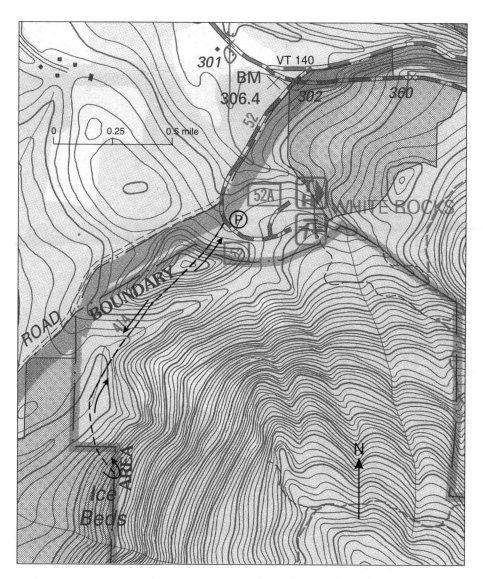

to the area and may be nesting on the cliffs, the White Rocks Trail may be closed during their nesting season; these beautiful endangered birds are easily disturbed from above. Please obey all posted signs, and refer to the introduction for more information about the falcons.

Return to the junction, and continue uphill along the Ice Beds Trail. Enjoy the good view back to White Rocks before you hike behind the ridge and have only limited views to the north. The trail is quite rocky in this section, so watch your step. The trail soon levels before descending toward, then away from, the base of White Rocks Cliff. At the double blaze, turn right, and begin a rocky descent. Follow the blazes along a series of small switchbacks as the trail becomes less

---

The summit of White Rocks

steep and more wooded. You begin to hear a brook to your left, and the air feels cool and damp.

After descending a few steps, you reach a junction with an old road, where you go left and downhill. Cross a brook on a small bridge, and follow along the valley floor. You soon cross the brook again, ascend slightly, and at 1.0 mile reach the Ice Beds, where the brook you have been following emerges from the base of the White Rocks Slide.

The USFS sign at the location reads:

A shattering of cheshire quartzite rock probably occurred during the ice age to create this rock slide. During the winter, ice and snow accumulate in the depths of the rock crevices. A continual downdraft of cold air in the shaded canyon helps preserve the ice and snow during the summer. The stream flowing from the rocks is fed by the melting ice. This keeps the water temperature at approximately 40 degrees throughout the summer.

After enjoying this cool, refreshing retreat (especially on a hot summer day!), hike back via the same trail to the picnic area.

4

Harmon Hill

Total distance: 3.4 miles

Hiking time: 3 hours

Vertical rise: 1,265 feet

Rating: Moderate

Maps: USGS 7.5' Woodford; 7.5' Bennington; 7.5' Pownal; 7.5' Stamford

This hike features an elaborate set of stone steps that ascend from the City Stream Valley, plus extensive views of Bennington and the Taconic Mountain Range. You also see the monument that commemorates the August 16, 1777, Battle of Bennington.

How to Get There

The trailhead is located at the Long Trail/Appalachian Trail (LT/AT) parking lot on the north side of VT 9, 4.5 miles east of US 7 in Bennington. Ample parking is available in this lot on the north side of the highway. A Green Mountain National Forest sign marks the trailhead on the south side of VT 9.

The Trail

Begin your hike by carefully crossing the highway and heading south on the white-blazed LT/AT. The trail enters the woods at a double blaze, turns right, and begins a long, steep ascent up stone steps. Climb quickly to a moss-covered boulder and outcrop; then traverse the first level section before climbing more stone steps. The road can be seen below you as you gain elevation. At 0.2 mile you begin a series of long switchbacks, moving from one set of steps to another as you ascend out of the valley.

You may be fortunate and see a garter snake sunning itself where the sun penetrates the high forest canopy. Remember that in most of Vermont, any snake you encounter is completely harmless. The very rare timber rattlesnake resides in the hills near New York's Lake George and is an endangered species in Vermont. Be warned,

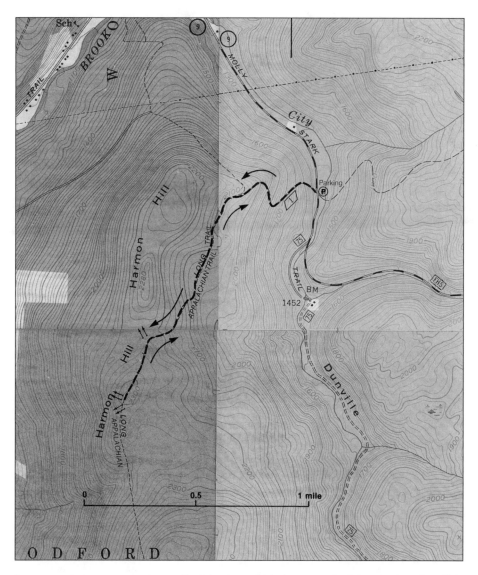

however, that garter snakes will defend themselves with a sharp bite if you try to pick them up. Safely enjoy snakes from a distance.

Light through the trees indicates that the climb is almost finished as you near the top of the ridge. At 0.6 mile the trail levels and descends slightly through a forest of primarily maple, birch, and oak trees, some of which have reached impressive size. This area provides a welcome contrast to the climb you just completed. You soon cross a tiny brook and enter a fern meadow. As you return to the forest, you reach a long set of puncheon, or bog bridges, at 1.0 mile. Cross another wet area on puncheon and stones, and ascend through a darker, denser wood.

The Long Trail going over Harmon Hill

BOB LINDEMANN

At 1.5 miles you come to another fern meadow with sunlight filtering through the trees. Soon the meadow opens up even more, and Bald Mountain ridge can be seen to the northwest. Raspberries growing along the trail should be ripe in late July. You pass through tall ferns before you reach the summit (elevation 2,325 feet) at 1.7 miles. Spur trails lead to views of Bennington, the battle monument, the Taconic Range, and Mount Anthony. The U.S. Forest Service keeps the large meadow open through the use of controlled burns.

To return, follow the same trail back down to your car. Be careful through the wet areas and on the steps, which are almost as difficult to descend as they are to ascend.

5

Haystack Mountain

Total distance: 4.8 miles

Hiking time: 3 hours

Vertical rise: 1,020 feet

Rating: Moderate

Map: USGS 7.5' Mount Snow

Rock outcroppings on the summit of Haystack Mountain provide beautiful views of southern Vermont and southwestern New Hampshire.

How to Get There

Care is needed to find the trailhead, which is located in the Chimney Hill development northwest of Wilmington. From the traffic light in Wilmington (0.0 mile), drive 1.1 miles west on VT 9. Turn right (north) onto Haystack Road, and at 1.4 miles, bear right, continuing to follow paved Haystack Road. At 2.35 miles, you reach an intersection where you turn left at a large Chimney Hill sign pointing the way to the Clubhouse and Chimney Hill Roads. At 2.5 miles, turn right onto unpaved Binney Brook Road. Continue uphill on Binney Brook Road by bearing left at the next three intersections. At 3.5 miles, turn right onto Upper Dam Road. Continue for a short distance on this road to a T-intersection at 3.6 miles where you turn left. At 3.8 miles you reach the trailhead, marked on your right with a U.S. Forest Service sign. Parking for about 10 cars is available along the road just beyond the trailhead. Please do not block driveways or park on private property.

The Trail

Your pathway, which follows an old road on easy to moderate grades, is sporadically marked with blue plastic diamonds. A sign indicating the Haystack Mountain Trail points up a driveway, adjacent to another road surfaced in crushed stone. Following

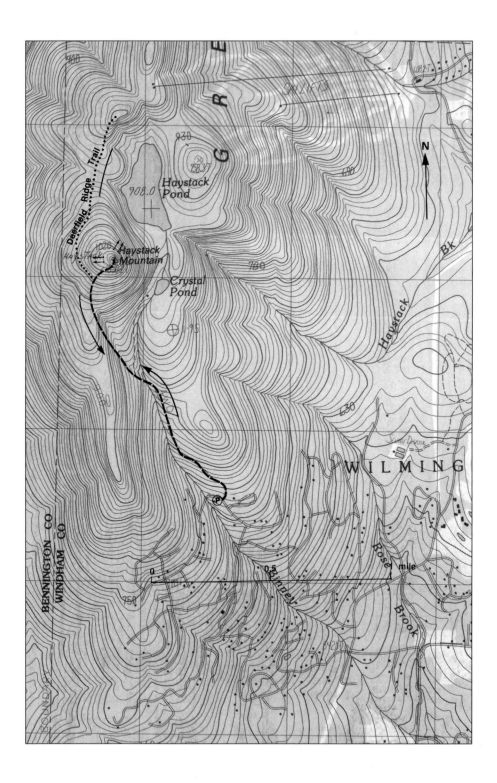

Looking south from Haystack Mountain

the trail uphill, the driveway soon bears right, and you should go straight. The trail then immediately turns left and soon intersects the crushed stone road. Turn right here, and pass by a yellow gate that blocks vehicles from driving up the road. Listen on your left for Binney Brook, which is the outlet for Haystack and Crystal Ponds.

At 0.75 mile, just after crossing Little Binney Brook, the trail turns left and follows the Deerfield Ridge Trail, used extensively in the winter by snowmobilers and cross-country skiers. This intersection is identified by signs marking the Wilmington Watershed Protection Area and prohibiting snowmobiles from continuing on the road, which eventually leads to Crystal and Haystack Ponds.

Descend slightly, and pass over some wet ground. The trail then curves right and ascends moderately on a rocky route for a short way before climbing more gradually along the ridge. You may notice that many beech and yellow birch trees in this area

sport contorted trunks and broken limbs. This is evidence of the harsh growing conditions found on this north-south ridge, which is nearly 3,000 feet in elevation. The trees here are subject to ice and high winds. At 1.6 miles you reach a small opening, with the summit of Haystack Mountain just visible straight ahead. Continue on a gentle ascent through a boggy section where the forest becomes increasingly evergreen. Pass a large rock outcrop on your left, and a minute or so later look for a trail leading uphill to the right. There is another watershed protection area sign at this intersection. Turn right and follow this winding trail as it ascends through a dense spruce-fir forest to the summit of Haystack Mountain at 2.4 miles.

Climb up and over two rock outcrops to a view overlooking the Deerfield Valley. Mount Monadnock in New Hampshire is straight ahead. Below is Haystack Pond, and to your far left is the summit of Mount Snow and its ski trails at the north end of the Deerfield Ridge. Just to the right of Mount Snow, on the far horizon, Killington Peak and the Coolidge Range may be visible to the north.

By walking to the right and negotiating a small cleft in the rock, you will come to two more vistas. One looks to the southeast, where you can spot Mount Wachusett, a rounded bump on an otherwise level horizon 60 miles away near Leominster, Massachusetts. The other vista, to the south, includes a view of Harriman Reservoir, or Lake Whitingham, the second-largest body of water completely within the state of Vermont. To its right are the 11 turbines of the Searsburg Wind Power Facility. The turbines are nearly 200 feet tall and generate enough electricity to power two thousand homes. The Searsburg facility, when constructed in 1997, was the largest of its kind in the East. Mount Greylock, with its War Memorial Tower, rises above the turbines. At 3,491 feet above sea level, Greylock is the highest point in Massachusetts. After enjoying the view, hike back down the same trail to your car.

6

Bald Mountain

Total distance: 3.4 miles

Hiking time: 3 hours

Vertical rise: 1,100 feet

Rating: Moderate

Map: USGS 7.5' x 15' Townshend

Bald Mountain, located in Townshend State Forest, offers excellent views of the surrounding area. The trail starts in Townshend State Park, which offers camping and picnicking. Nearby is the U.S. Army Corps of Engineers's Townshend Lake Recreation Area, where you can swim and picnic before or after your hike. On your way to the trail, you pass the Scott Covered Bridge, which spans the West River. The bridge, built in 1870, is composed of three separate spans. The northern span, a town lattice truss that was later strengthened, though unsuccessfully, with laminated wooden arches, is 165.7 feet long—the longest single span of any covered bridge in Vermont.

How to Get There

To reach the Townshend State Park, drive 2.0 miles north of Townshend Village on VT 30 to the Townshend Dam. Turn left (west), and cross the spillway on a narrow bridge. Just past the dam and recreation access (0.0 mile), the road reaches a T-intersection at 0.2 mile. Turn left, and pass the Scott Covered Bridge at 0.8 mile. Bear right at the bridge, and continue parallel to the West River until you reach the park entrance at 1.4 miles. Parking is available in a small lot just before the park building. Walk to the building, where a day-use fee is charged.

The Trail

You begin your hike in Townshend State Park, the site of a Civilian Conservation

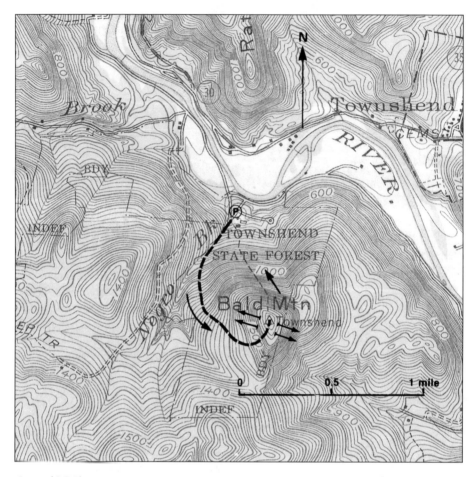

Corps (CCC) camp during the Depression. The CCC constructed the picnic area and campground at the park and also built the stone caretaker's dwelling and attached picnic shelter. This structure was placed on the National Register of Historic Places in 2001.

Cross the road to the right of the park building. Descend on a short spur trail to campsite 25, where the trailhead is marked with a sign and very large blue blazes. Take the trail over Negro Brook on a bridge constructed by the Vermont Youth Conservation Corps in 1990, and turn left. Begin climbing on an old truck road built by the

CCC in the mid-1930s. Floodwaters from the 1938 hurricane caused extensive damage to the road and its four bridges, and the road was never rebuilt.

The road closely follows Negro Brook as it tumbles down the side of Bald Mountain, and you should take time to enjoy the brook's pretty cascades and pools. Watch for a double blue blaze, which signals a turn to the left. Here, at the remains of an old bridge abutment, you cross the brook. The trail bears left at an old road junction and ascends away from the brook. At 0.6 mile the trail bears right to avoid a logging area, then parallels and crosses a logging road.

The ranger station at Townshend State Park

Ascend along the hillside, covered with small boulders, into an open hemlock forest. Follow the blazes carefully in this area, as the lack of vegetation on the forest floor makes the trail difficult to discern. The trail bears sharply right and continues on easy grades through several wet areas.

The trail, now nearly level, joins an old road that leads up a wet, rocky draw. At 1.1 miles you pass by a large rock outcrop on the left and cross a brook. Another old road intersects the trail, which now follows the brook bed. Leave the brook bed and walk on bedrock. Turn left at the edge of a swamp where red spruce and speckled alder are found, and begin a steep ascent up the peak. The dry soils, coarse-grained and shallow, result in a forest of stunted red oak and white pine with a lovely open, grassy understory. Rock outcrops are scattered across the forest floor. Continue on the steep but quite open trail to the 1,680-foot summit at 1.7 miles. A sign directs you to a southeastern view that includes Mount Monadnock in New Hampshire and the West River Valley below you. The western view includes Stratton and Bromley Mountains. Look for foundation footings of an old fire tower between the two overlooks. A fire station was established on Bald Mountain in 1912. This spot was one of the earliest sites in Vermont used as a forest fire lookout. The CCC built a steel tower on the summit in the early 1930s. In 1950 the tower was relocated to Mount Olga in Wilmington (see hike 1).

After enjoying the views, return via the same route to your car.

Note: In 1996, the eastern return leg of the old loop trail, which continued over the summit and down the north side of the mountain, was closed because of severe erosion.

Bald Mountain

7

Antone Mountain

Total distance: 5 miles

Hiking time: 3 hours

Vertical rise: 890 feet

Rating: Moderate

Map: USGS 7.5' Pawlet

This hike in southwestern Vermont follows some of the 26 miles of trails at the Merck Forest and Farmland Center, a nonprofit outdoor educational facility that also contains a small diversified farm, fields, hardwood forests, and several small ponds and streams. It offers a variety of educational programs, including astronomy, forest management, wildflower and bird identification, and low-impact camping.

How to Get There

The center can be reached from East Rupert. From VT 30 (0.0 mile), follow VT 315 west 2.4 miles to the height-of-land and a Merck Forest sign on your left. Turn left onto the dirt road, and continue to a visitors center and a parking area at 2.9 miles. An information board adjacent to the visitors center includes area rules (no mountain bikes; no unleashed dogs) as well as trail maps that are available with a donation to help cover the center's expenses.

The Trail

The unblazed trail, which follows old roads, starts from the information board. Follow the dirt road on level grades until you reach a field with a sugarhouse on your right. The caretaker's cabin is on your left, and at the road intersection ahead there are picnic tables, a barn, and a small natural history museum. Take time to visit the museum's interesting exhibits on area wildlife and forests.

Continue your hike on the Old Towne Road by going straight at the intersection.

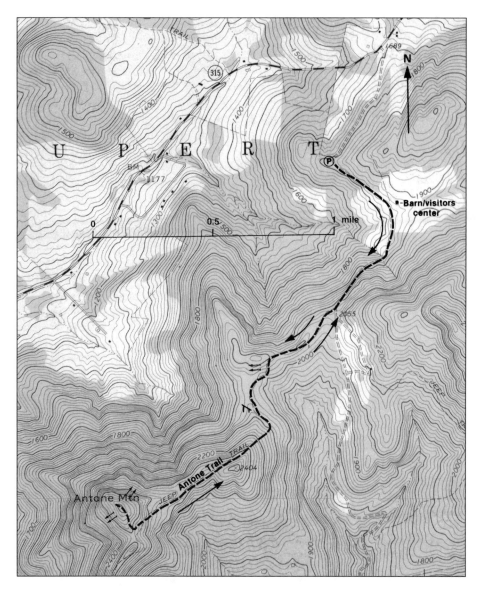

This is the oldest road in Merck Forest, built by Ebenezer Smith in 1781 to provide access between his home on the mountain and the town highway. The most recent roads are used for logging and sugaring, which help support the educational center. Old Towne Road passes several fields, descends for a short distance, and then ascends on easy grades. Enjoy the nice views to the north and northwest of New York's Adirondack Mountains.

Stay on Old Towne Road through the Gallup Road intersection on your left and then the McCormick Trail intersection on your right at 0.5 mile. Hike up a short, steep grade, and pass a small clearing on your right as the road levels again. The Old Towne Road turns left, and you come to a well-marked junction with Lodge Road on your left and Mount Antone Road on your right. Turn right onto Mount Antone Road along easy grades on top of the ridge, and then descend to Clark's Clearing, a log landing, at 1.3 miles. You pass the McCormick Trail junction on your right and a small lean-to for firewood on your left. Look for berry bushes in two small clearings, where you can feast on ripe berries in late July while enjoying views of Antone Mountain.

Follow the trail into the woods until you come to Clark's Clearing shelter and trail intersection. The Clark's Clearing Road bears left, and a spur trail bears right. Continue straight on the Mount Antone Road up a steep grade to the top of the ridge. The road levels and starts an easy, winding descent. At 1.9 miles you reach the Wade Lot Road junction on your left. Continue on Antone Road and hike past the Lookout Road junction, again on your left, and climb the mountainside on moderate grades past the Beebe Pond Trail and Masters Mountain Trail junction. The Mount Antone Trail continues to the right up a steep grade to the summit (elevation 2,610 feet) at 2.5 miles. There are views to the east and northeast of the visitors center's barn, Dorset Peak, Woodlawn Mountain, and the Pawlet area. A trail beyond the summit leads downhill to another lookout, with good views of the Adirondack Mountains, eastern New York, and the Rupert and Pawlet areas.

After enjoying the views, hike back to the summit and retrace your steps to the parking area.

8

Bromley Mountain

Total distance: 5.0 miles

Hiking time: 3.5 hours

Vertical rise: 890 feet

Rating: Moderate

Map: USGS 7.5' Danby; 7.5' Peru

Bromley Mountain is a ski area mountain, with chairlifts and buildings and other facilities associated with downhill skiing on its summit. None of this should keep you from walking up Bromley, however. The Long Trail/Appalachian Trail (LT/AT) from Mad Tom Notch south to the 3,260-foot summit is an extremely pleasant route. Except for two short sections, the trail is never steep or rocky. Any climbing you do alternates with level sections of trail, and your route is punctuated with attractive stretches of forests filled with spruce and fir. Once at the summit, a wooden observation tower offers 360-degree views of the Green and Taconic Mountains.

How to Get There

From VT 11 between Londonderry and Manchester, follow signs to the village of Peru. In the center of the village, turn north onto Hapgood Pond Road at the Congregational Church (0.0 mile), and at 0.9 mile turn left onto North Road, which soon becomes dirt. Turn left again at 1.7 miles onto Mad Tom Notch Road, and follow it to the top of the hill and the LT/AT crossing at 3.9 miles. A parking area for a dozen cars is just past the trail on the left. The last 1.1 miles of Mad Tom Notch Road are not plowed in winter.

The Trail

Follow the white blazes of the LT/AT south through a wet area in a mixed forest. After a few minutes, the trail begins climbing gently through a hardwood forest of birch, beech,

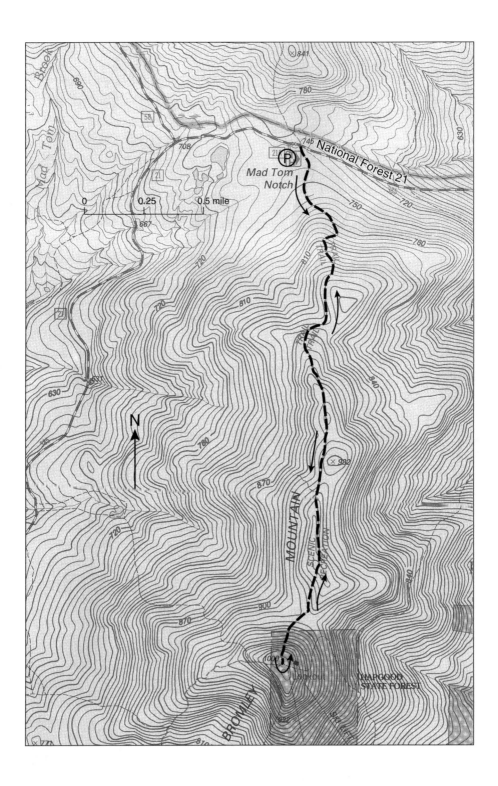

JEFF NUGENT

Descending the AT/LT on Bromley Mountain

and maple. Make several turns as you follow overgrown woods roads for short distances on your ascent of the ridge.

After passing a large boulder on the right, the trail levels out for a ways before ascending gently once again to another flat section. The hardwood forest here has shorter trees, a more open canopy, and a brushy understory. The trail then enters a lovely section filled with spruce and fir. Mosses, ferns, and wood sorrel carpet the forest floor as plank walkways, called puncheon, and stepping-stones take you across boggy areas.

Several sections of gradual ups and downs bring you to one short, steep uphill that tops out next to a small, flat-topped rock on Bromley's north peak at 2.1 miles. The rock is a perfect height for sitting upon, and you may wish to rest here before continuing on over the only truly steep portion of your hike.

The trail now suddenly drops over rocks and stone steps toward a col at the base of Bromley's summit. You descend through several brushy openings in the forest before the trail becomes level. Look to your left for an orange stake and paint blazes that mark the property boundary between U.S. Forest Service land, which you have been on since the beginning of your walk, and the Hapgood State Forest, which encompasses the top of Bromley Mountain.

Now begin a short, steady ascent to the grassy summit of Bromley Mountain at 2.5 miles. A wooden observation tower, which you can climb for 360-degree views over the mountains of southern Vermont, is straight ahead.

While you're looking out from the summit, consider what the area was like 200 years ago. It must have been a tough existence in the mountain town of Peru. The original name of the town, like the mountain today, was Bromley, but residents felt the name was rather dull sounding and indicative of poverty. In 1804, the people of Bromley voted to change the name of their town to Peru, hoping the new name would be associated with the wealth and treasures of that South American country and would bring prosperity to the area. Interestingly, it is the original name Bromley, as in the mountain and the ski area, that has brought change and opportunity to the area unimaginable to the early nineteenth-century residents.

Return to the 21st century, and follow the LT/AT north back to your car.

9

Little Rock Pond and Green Mountain

Total distance: 7-mile loop

Hiking time: 4 hours

Vertical rise: 960 feet

Rating: Moderately strenuous

Map: USGS 7.5' Wallingford

This hike, which provides a nice variation from the usual out-and-back trail, allows you to enjoy both mountain trails and a beautiful pond. Leave a full day for this journey to give yourself adequate time to enjoy the pond, as well as some wonderful views.

How to Get There

To reach the trail, take US 7 to its junction with U.S. Forest Service (USFS) Road 10 in Mount Tabor. Turn east onto USFS Road 10, also called the Danby-Landgrove Road. Cross the railroad tracks, and go by the USFS Mount Tabor Work Center. Follow the road uphill, passing a water fountain on the left side at the last home before entering the Green Mountain National Forest. The source of the water is a spring on the west of the valley; its function was to cool off wagonloads of still-hot charcoal brought down off the mountain to stoke the local iron furnaces. Pass a sign at 0.9 mile that indicates you have entered the White Rocks National Recreational Area. Cross the silver bridge, and follow the road up the mountain, passing beautiful stone culverts built by the Civilian Conservation Corps crews from the camp where the Mount Tabor Work Center now sits. At 2.7 miles, you reach Big Branch Overlook. The road turns to dirt at 3.0 miles. You soon reach the paved Long Trail (LT) parking area at 3.2 miles, where there is space for approximately 20 cars.

The Trail

Cross the road, and follow the white-blazed Long Trail/Appalachian Trail (LT/AT) north to

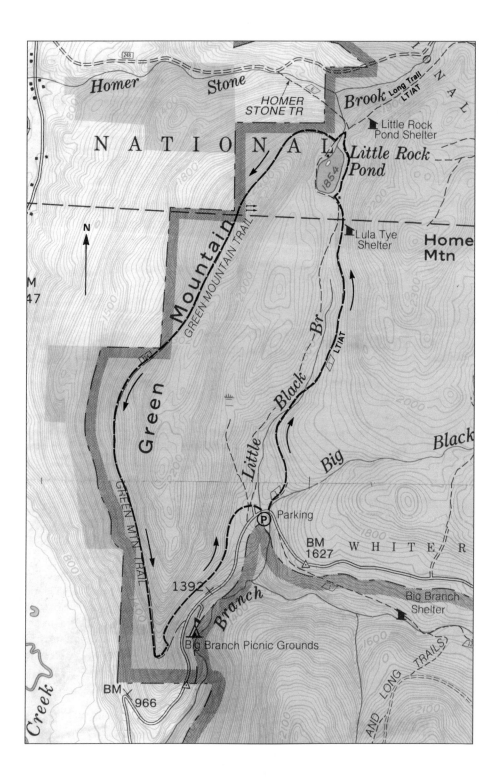

Homer Stone

248

HOMER STONE TR

67

Brook Long Trail LT/AT

▲ Little Rock Pond Shelter

Little Rock Pond

1854

Home Mtn

▲ Lula Tye Shelter

N A T I O N A L

N

M 47

GREEN MOUNTAIN TRAIL

Green Mountain

Little Black Br

LT/AT

1800

1500

2200

2000

Black

Big

GREEN MTN TRAIL

P Parking

BM 1627

W H I T E R

1800

1392

Branch

△

Big Branch Picnic Grounds

Big Branch Shelter

BM 966

△

1600

AND LONG TRAILS

18

Creek

Little Rock Pond's Island

Little Rock Pond. The signpost at the trailhead indicates a distance of 2 miles to the pond, your first stop on this hike. The beginning of this trail, which starts as a gradual climb, is strewn with bricks and black soot from an old charcoal kiln. Enter some mixed hardwoods, and start to leave the brook behind. Follow an old roadway parallel to the brook on your left, and soon cross the brook on a steel I-beam bridge, set in the 1940s, at 0.6 mile.

The trail swings right after the bridge

and continues to follow, then cross, the brook. By 1.0 mile, the brook is considerably smaller as you cross a wet area on puncheon. The trail then switches from a roadway into a more rugged path with numerous slippery wet areas, so be sure to watch your step. At 1.8 miles you reach a spur trail on your right that goes to the Lula Tye Shelter. In 1972, members of the Student Conservation Association moved this shelter from Little Rock Pond to its current location to reduce hiker impact on the pond area. The shelter is named in memory of the woman who served as Green Mountain Club corresponding secretary from 1926 to 1955.

A sign at this junction says the pond is 0.2 mile farther along the LT/AT. The trail becomes very rocky during this next section, so be careful of your footing until you reach the south end of the pond at 2.0 miles.

Little Rock Pond, up to 60 feet deep in places, is one of the most popular day- and overnight-use areas on the LT/AT. A good fishing spot, the pond is annually stocked with brook trout. Beavers frequent the area, and moose have occasionally been sighted along the pond shore. Careful management is required to preserve the area's natural beauty and fragile shoreline environment. Because of the area's popularity, a Green Mountain Club caretaker is stationed at the site during the hiking season to assist hikers, maintain the local trails and campsites, and compost sewage to protect water quality. A small camping fee is charged.

Follow the Little Rock Pond Loop Trail around the west side of the pond. This was the original trail route around the pond. Cross over an impressive ledge above the pond, and then descend to pass the pond's island. A bridge once led to the island, where the trail shelter used to be located. It was relocated away from the island in 1972, when heavy use threatened the island's vegetation and the pond's water quality.

At 2.4 miles, reach the Green Mountain Trail, and turn left to follow it uphill away from the pond. Switchback up the ridge, and climb to the right of a long pointed rock outcrop that resembles a dinosaur's back. Occasional views along the trail remind you how far you have climbed above the pond. At 3.0 miles, you reach a ledge with views down to the pond. Return to a wooded ridge walk, climb over a steep rock face, and reach the unsigned Pond View junction. Hike straight ahead for 100 yards to spectacular views of the pond and valley below.

From the junction, the trail takes a sharp right into a spruce forest, with minor ascents and switchbacks. Pass through a series of rock shelves with several short side trails to the left for views; note especially a spur at 3.7 miles. Back on the main trail, which now resembles an old road, descend through some mixed hardwoods. The trail is quite wide in this section. Descend and ascend short distances through two saddles, continuing through spruce forest and then a mix of spruce and white birch. There is a signed spur to the left for a vista with an excellent view. Continue trending downhill through evergreens and, after a while, mixed hardwoods and lots of ferns. Throughout your hike, note the spring wildflowers—clintonia, bunchberry, jack-in-the-pulpit, trillium, and lady slipper.

The end of the first major descent is reached at 4.5 miles, where you turn left and continue through mature hardwoods. Be careful to watch for blazes in this area. Continue your descent, then travel through a level area and descend again until you cross a brook at 5.2 miles. Enter a much younger hardwood forest, climb briefly again, then level off. You soon reach a very unusual old road cut out of the hillside. Enjoy views of the valley through the trees along the road. Traverse the side of the mountain, mostly on a gentle downhill, but with one steeper section. As you cross a rock slide, take time to notice that the area uphill is predominantly hardwood, whereas the valley below is all softwood; the road forms the dividing line. The trail then swings around the edge of the ridge, and you begin to hear Big Branch Brook. The trail now is fairly level, following the old road.

At 6.4 miles you reach another trail junction, where you bear left onto the Green Mountain Connector Trail to return to your car. The trail straight ahead leads downhill to another parking lot and USFS Road 10. As you turn left and return to the woods, pass among some beech trees, and descend along an old road. At the bottom of the hill you begin to see USFS Road 10 on the right as you cross a wet overgrown area parallel to it. At 7.0 miles, cross a gravel road, pass through another wet overgrown area, and descend to the road. Turn left, and return to the parking lot.

10

Okemo Mountain

Total distance: 6.0 miles; 6.5 miles with summit loop

Hiking time: 4 hours

Vertical rise: 1,950 feet

Rating: Moderate

Map: USGS 7.5' Ludlow; 7.5' Mount Holly

Okemo is a mountain of contrasts, with a ski area on one side and a wilderness hiking trail on the other. Built in the summers of 1991 to 1993 by the Youth Conservation Corps, this blue-blazed trail ascends 3.0 miles from the village of Healdville (named for its first postmaster) to the 3,343-foot summit of Mount Okemo. On the summit you will find a fire tower, complete with a 360-degree view of the surrounding region.

How to Get There

From its junction with VT 140 in East Wallingford, follow VT 103 east until reaching the gravel Station Road at 6.4 miles. Turn right onto Station Road, and follow it until reaching a grade crossing of the Green Mountain Railroad near the hamlet of Healdville at 7.2 miles. A signed parking lot with room for 10 cars is located just past the tracks on the left, at the former site of the Healdville Station. Be sure to check out the trailhead information board.

From the east, follow VT 103 west from its junction with VT 100 north of Ludlow. Reach Station Road at 2.75 miles. Turn right onto Station Road to the railroad crossing and the trailhead parking lot at 3.5 miles.

The Trail

From the parking lot, follow the blue-blazed trail parallel to the railroad tracks, following an old woods road across a small bridge in 50 feet. Turn right from the railroad, and climb gently. Cross a bridge over a brook at 0.2 mile, pass a cascade at 0.6 mile, and

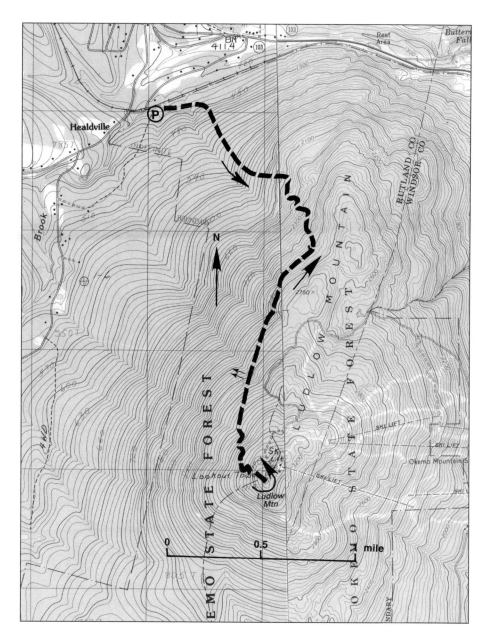

cross a small brook at 0.7 mile as you gently ascend on the old woods road. The mix of dense, small hardwoods that surrounds you is an indication of past logging in this area. Leave the woods road and brook you have been following, ascend on moderate to easy grades on some switchbacks, and pass glacial boulders and rock outcrops. At 1.5 miles, the grade levels as you reach a plateau. You have climbed about 1,100 feet,

The view from the Okemo Mountain firetower

more than half the climb, and you have gone half the distance to the top. Notice how much more mature the forest is now. Maples begin to yield to yellow birch and occasional hemlock and spruce.

A sign at 1.9 miles indicates you are 1 mile from the summit. A small split boulder with embedded quartz is just right of the trail. Here, an unmarked trail ascends 0.2 mile to the paved summit road. You can make this part of a loop trip, described below. Descend gradually, cross a rock-filled gully, and pass by glaciated rock outcrops as the trail gets steeper and you pass through a grove of white birch. At 2.3 miles, you reach an overlook to the west with VT 103 below you and (right to left) Salt Ash Mountain, Shrewsbury Peak, Killington Peak, Little Killington, Mendon

Peak, and the Taconics in the distance. Beyond the overlook, ascend again as the forest changes to spruce and fir (with ferns and wood sorrel on its floor) and the trail becomes rockier. Pass 20 feet right of a tiny marsh at 2.7 miles, enjoy a short level stretch in evergreens and striped maples, and then climb steeply. At 2.9 miles take a sharp left turn through a switchback to a northern view of Killington Peak. You can also see most of what you could see at the lower lookout, plus Lake Ninevah and Echo Lake (which locals called Plymouth Pond), near the village of Tyson.

Isaac Tyson Jr., originally from Baltimore, Maryland, discovered iron in this region in 1835. He developed the Tyson Furnace into what was once one of the most productive iron regions in New England.

After enjoying the view, continue on the now nearly level trail to an overgrown area where you will find the chimney, foundation, and wood remains of a forest ranger's cabin. Just beyond the cabin site, look for a sign on a tree that points right to the summit fire tower. Follow the fire tower trail 100 feet to the tower, still complete with a roof, at 3.0 miles.

The tower gives a 360-degree view of southern Vermont. Below you is the Okemo Ski Area, east is Mount Ascutney with its antennae, north is Killington Peak, directly south are Stratton and Bromley Mountains, and southwest are Dorset Peak and the Taconic Range. After resting and enjoying the beautiful view, return via the same trails to your car. Alternatively, you may choose a summit loop leading past several fine views. This is especially worthwhile if you don't want to climb the tower or want to find a scenic picnic spot out of the wind.

To make the loop, descend the first 100 feet the way you came, then continue down the broad path toward the parking lot. At 0.1 mile, however, turn right onto a dirt service road, and follow it 250 feet to the top of a ski lift that gives a fine northeast to southeast view, including Croydon Mountain in New Hampshire, Mount Ascutney on the Connecticut River, and the village of Ludlow. Continue on the service road, which doubles as the Buckhorn Ski Trail, over the ridge and down past the Summit Lodge to the top of another lift, 0.5 mile from the summit. Here, the easterly views are almost as good as from the tower: Mendon Peak, Little Killington, Killington Peak, Salt Ash Mountain, Echo Lake and Lake Rescue on VT 100, Croydon Mountain in New Hampshire, Mount Ascutney on the Connecticut River, and the village of Ludlow. Descending from the top of the lift, turn right from the service road onto a ski trail in 100 feet, follow it for 200 feet, and turn left into the woods on a wide but unmarked trail. Climb gently over a ridge, and reach the parking lot 0.7 mile from the summit by this route. (If you go direct, it is 0.4 mile from the summit.)

From the gravel parking lot, follow the paved summit road and reach Ludlow Overlook at 0.9 mile. It gives views from Killington to Ascutney. Continue down to the Mount Holly Overlook at 1.2 miles, with views from northwest to north, including most of the Coolidge Range. At 1.4 miles, at the farthest east point of a gentle curve in the summit road, near a 1-foot diameter maple, turn left into the woods on a path that may be marked with orange surveyor's ribbon. At 1.6 miles from the summit, reach the Healdville Trail at the sign mentioned above. From here, it is another 1.9 miles back to the parking lot. You will have hiked 3.5 miles down from the tower, for a total trip of 6.5 miles. This alternate round trip should take you about 4¼ hours, not counting time to enjoy the views.

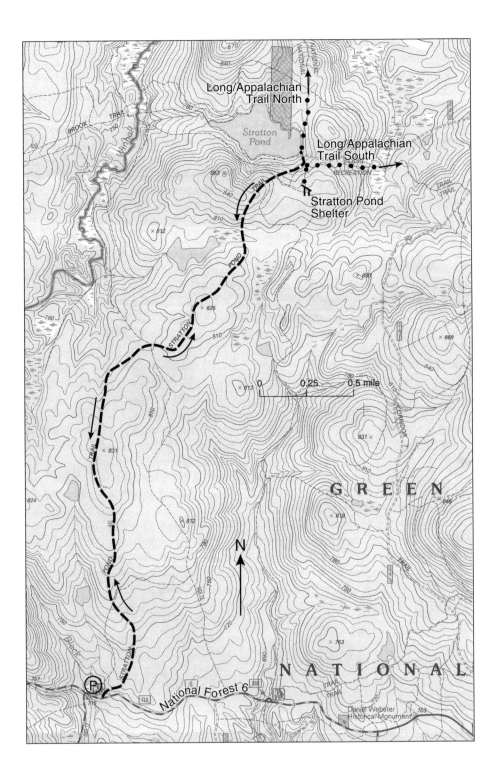

Long/Appalachian
Trail North

Stratton
Pond

Long/Appalachian
Trail South

Stratton Pond
Shelter

0   0.25   0.5 mile

N

G R E E N

N A T I O N A L

National Forest 6

Daniel Webster
Historical Monument

11

Stratton Pond

Total distance: 7.8 miles

Hiking time: 4½ hours

Vertical rise: 660 feet

Rating: Moderate

Map: USGS 7.5' Stratton Mountain

This long but almost level hike leads to Stratton Pond. The route is easy walking. Much of the path you follow is devoid of rocks and tree roots, thanks in part to the careful trail work that has been done. The trip can be extended by 1.4 miles by following a network of trails around the pond. Stratton Pond is located just east of the 15,680-acre Lye Brook Wilderness. There are few trails through this heavily forested wilderness, but several lakes, streams, and bogs dot the landscape. The wilderness contains beautiful waterfalls and meadows, as well as the remnants of old logging railroads and sawmills. "The Burning," the site of a large fire around the turn of the 20th century, is located in the western portion of the wilderness. It is a popular spot for wildlife, such as wild turkey, white-tailed deer, and black bear.

How to Get There

The trail is located on the north side of the Stratton-Arlington Road (also known as the Kelley Stand Road). From VT 100 in West Wardsboro (0.0 mile), drive 8.2 miles west on Stratton-Arlington Road to a parking area on the right side of the road. This is just before the intersection with U.S. Forest Service (USFS) Road 71. A wooden USFS sign and information board marks the trailhead.

The Trail

This blue-blazed trail follows the former route of the Long Trail/Appalachian Trail (LT/AT). Note the extensive trail work—

The North Shore Trail on Stratton Pond

including water bars, puncheon, and turn-piking—along your route. Puncheon are plank walkways constructed to span wet or boggy areas. Turnpiking involves creating a hardened, slightly elevated trail bed over soft ground by piling soil between logs or rocks placed along both sides of the trail Water bars are found on steeper sections of trail, where logs or shingled stones are laid diagonally across the trail to support ditches that divert rainfall runoff from the trail to prevent erosion.

Begin your hike across puncheon and over turnpiking through a young beech and softwood forest. The trail, now resembling a boardwalk through the woods, ascends slightly and crosses several wet areas on puncheon. Pass through a section of white birches, and come to an open area with ferns. At 1.5 miles, follow puncheon across another wet area, and enter a birch forest. This area is quite beautiful on a sunny day, with sunlight filtering through the trees.

After a long stretch of puncheon, you cross an old road at 2.3 miles. This road coincides with the Catamount Trail, a cross-country ski trail running the entire length of Vermont. Some of the trail's most remote sections are in the Stratton and Somerset areas.

Enter a dark, dense softwood forest with more puncheon before returning to a sunnier, more open hardwood forest. As you begin a gradual ascent, notice the large stumps that indicate the size of the trees that once grew in this area. Cross another wet area on puncheon, and look to your right for a large birch with roots engulfing a boulder. Continue your hike through a small softwood forest, across more puncheon, and then through a forest now composed of white birch and a spruce understory. The forest becomes dominated by hardwoods once again before you pass a large moss-covered boulder.

At 3.8 miles you cross a small brook on

stepping-stones. Soon after, you come to a trail junction. Your route, which continues on the Stratton Pond Trail, turns left, but you may wish to take a short detour by turning right and walking 100 feet up the side trail to see the impressive Stratton Pond Shelter. This two-story post-and-beam shelter was built in 1999 and can sleep 24 people. From the trail junction, descend a rocky, wet, old logging road to the junction of the LT/AT. A USFS sign indicates that Stratton Mountain is 2.6 miles east from this junction.

Turn left, and follow the LT/AT north to the shore of Stratton Pond at 3.9 miles. The pond, where you can swim and fish, is 30 feet deep at its deepest point and averages 10 feet deep overall. Most of the pond and surrounding lands were acquired by the USFS in 1985. Stratton Pond, the largest body of water on the LT, is one of the highest overnight-use areas on the trail. There are more than 2,000 overnight hikers at the pond between Memorial Day and Columbus Day. Until recently, two shelters at the pond's shoreline focused much of the overnight use at the water's edge. Trampling of shoreline vegetation, degradation of water quality as a result of poor waste disposal, and the loss of a sense of solitude on the pond caused the land and trail managers to reexamine camping at Stratton Pond.

Today, a tenting area with tent platforms is located away from the pond's edge, as is the new shelter. Composting toilets are used at both sites to protect water quality. A Green Mountain Club caretaker is stationed at the site during the hiking season to assist hikers, maintain the trails and campsites, and compost sewage. Please follow the caretaker's instructions to help protect this valuable natural area.

The clearing where the LT reaches the pond shoreline is the legacy of a popular backcountry lodge, Willis Ross Camp, which burned in 1972. If time permits, you may wish to circle the pond. From the clearing, you can follow the Lye Brook Trail west along the south shore of the pond, cross the pond's outlet at the opposite shore, and then complete your circuit by taking the North Shore Trail east back to the LT. Turn right onto the LT, and return to the clearing, completing a 1.4-mile loop. The walk will treat you to a view across the water of Stratton Mountain and a traverse of a wetland area. After exploring the pond area, return to Kelley Stand Road via the LT south from the pond and Stratton Pond Trail.

12

Mount Ascutney

Total distance: 5.8 miles

Hiking time: 4½ hours

Vertical rise: 2,060 feet

Rating: Strenuous

Map: USGS 7.5' Mount Ascutney

Mount Ascutney is an unusual monadnock (a hill or mountain of resistant rock) located near Windsor. The mountain's granite and related gabbro-diorite and syenite rock is the remains of an underground upswelling of molten White Mountain magma through the native metamorphic rocks during the collision between the North American and European plates, before part of the European plate detached from the rest and became what is now New Hampshire. This monadnock has withstood the erosion and glaciation that has worn away the softer rocks of the surrounding piedmont peneplain, an area near the foot of a mountain that has been almost reduced to a plain by erosion.

The mountain derives its name from the word *Ascutegnik,* meaning "meeting of the waters," which was originally the name of an Abenaki settlement where the Sugar River joins the Connecticut River. The Abenaki words for the mountain itself were *Cas-Cad-Nac*, meaning "mountain of the rocky summit."

The first trail on Mount Ascutney may have been opened in 1825. In 1858, a trail that was almost a road was opened along much of the route of the present Windsor Trail. In 1883, a summer-long forest fire burned away stretches of this trail. Great boulders lined the trails, and charred tree trunks and ash were everywhere. The Ascutney Mountain Association was formed in 1903 to relocate the damaged part of the Windsor Trail and rebuild the destroyed stone hut on top of the mountain. In 1898,

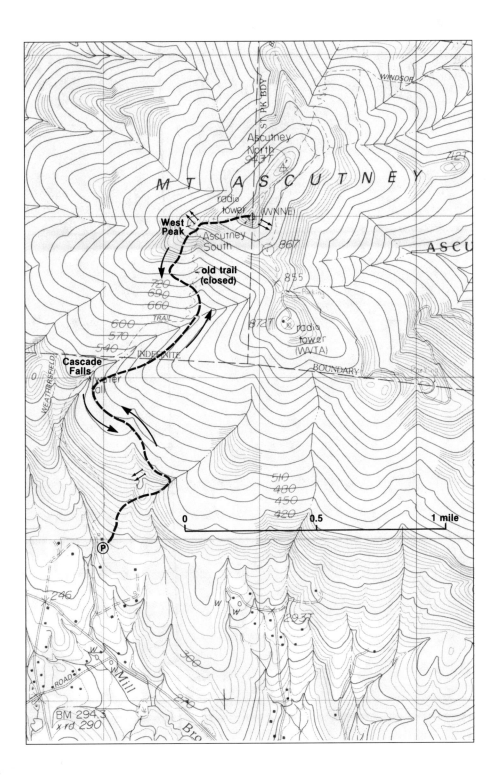

Lady's-slipper

the Brownsville Trail was opened, followed by the Weathersfield Trail in 1906.

In 1920, a ranger cabin and summit fire-watch tower were constructed on the mountain. Around 1940, the Civilian Conservation Corps (CCC) built a new steel tower, which was abandoned as a fire tower in the 1950s. The tower remained standing until the mid-1980s. In 1989, a new viewing tower just above treetop level was built about 300 feet north of the summit.

The building of a road in 1934 by the CCC, as well as the great hurricane of 1938, created so much debris and so many trail problems that by 1966 only the Weathersfield Trail could easily be found. In that year the Herbert Ogdens (junior and senior) located, cleared, blazed, signed, measured, and mapped the Windsor Trail. In 1967, the Ascutney Trails Association (ATA) was formed to continue their work; it still maintains the trails on the mountain. Its interesting 47-page *Mount Ascutney Guide*, describing all four main trails up Ascutney, their history, and more, is available from the Ascutney Trails Association, P.O. Box 147, Windsor VT 05089, for $5. Please consider joining the ATA after benefiting from its work. Dues are $10 for families, $2 for people younger than 18, and $5 for people 18 and older.

Because of several antennas, the summit is not as interesting as the west peak, which is more secluded and used as a hang-glider launching site.

How to Get There

Take exit 8 (Ascutney) off I-91 to VT 131 west (0.0 mile). Drive 3.3 miles to Cascade Falls Road, and turn right (north). Bear left at the fork, and continue to a right turn at 3.6 miles. Drive up the short steep hill to the 15-car parking lot and the information board. The state of Vermont and the ATA built the trailhead and parking area in 1989.

The Trail

From the information board at the left rear end of the parking lot, take the blue-blazed Weathersfield Trail, which ascends some small log stairs and enters the woods. Swing right along easy grades, cross a small brook, ascend moderately, and cross just above Little Cascade Falls. In tall evergreens, continue your ascent to a deep, mossy rock cleft into which a little brook falls. This flume is 0.5 mile from the trailhead. Hike out the other side on rock and log steps. Now on easier grades, pass several overlooks at 0.6 mile. The trail crosses an old logging road and proceeds almost level for a while. This break is a rarity on this mountain, where most trails climb ceaselessly. Descending slightly through spruce and hemlock, the trail leads to the top of Crystal Cascade at 1.2 miles, where there is a good view to the south.

The geology of Crystal Cascade is unusual. This 84-foot, nearly sheer cliff is a rare example of a ring dike, formed by the upward flow of magma into a somewhat circular fissure. The molten rock made its way through overlying sedimentary rocks; however, the fledgling volcano lacked the thrust necessary to reach the surface, and all the White Mountain magma cooled underground. Erosion and glaciation wore away much of the overlying bedrock, exposing the igneous edge of the ring dike. The rocks at the border of the newly formed pluton (any body of igneous rock solidified far below the earth's surface) were metamorphosed by the extreme heat of the magma. This contact zone is clearly visible at the base of Crystal Cascade, where a second bedrock shows as a gray mass. Evidence of the ring dike formation can also be found at the top of the Cascades. Chunks of the surrounding bedrock were constantly consumed by the magma as it moved upward. However, pieces that were only partially absorbed when the magma cooled are visible in the little cascades above the cliff. After crossing the bottom of the valley and the brook, climb a small bank, and turn right onto an old woods road. You are now on the original 1906 route of the Weathersfield Trail, which is blazed in white, so expect a combination of white and blue blazes to the summit. Continue on the road past several rock outcrops to Halfway Brooks at 1.7 miles. Turn left from the old route, and follow the sign's instructions to stay on the trail and not take shortcuts as you ascend the steep ridge. Erosion here is a serious problem that you can help control by staying on the trail. Still climbing, you pass exposed rock outcrops, where you can rest and enjoy the views. Swing right through some stunted birches, and return to the woods on easier grades.

At 2.3 miles, make a sharp right turn at Gus's Lookout (elevation 2,690 feet), a series of large rock outcrops with views of the Connecticut River Valley and the summit ridge. The lookout was named for Augustus Aldrich, a charter ATA member and trail worker, who died in 1974 on Mount Katah-din at age 86. Below and above the lookout are two bypasses to avoid the slippery rocks in wet weather.

Return to the woods, pass a large boulder on a switchback through a fern-filled white birch grove, and reach West Peak Spring. Climb moderately on switchbacks to a trail junction at 2.6 miles. A spur to the left leads 0.1 mile to the 2,940-foot west peak with views of the Green Mountain Range. A second spur leads to a hang-glider takeoff ramp. Back on the main trail, climb moderately and then steeply to the ridge. To the right, the antennae-covered 3,150-foot summit is reached at 2.9 miles. To the left, a white-blazed trail leads past the observation tower and then splits. The right fork descends to a parking lot at the top of the Ascutney Road. The left fork continues north to the Stone Hut, 0.2 mile north of the summit. There are several trails connecting points of interest on the mountaintop, described and mapped in the ATA's *Mount Ascutney Guide*.

Return to the junction south of the observation tower, and hike back down the trail to your car.

13

Griffith Lake and Baker Peak

Total distance: 8.2 miles

Hiking time: 5¹⁄₂ hours

Vertical rise: 2,340 feet

Rating: Strenuous

Map: USGS 7.5' Wallingford

The first 3.5 miles of this strenuous hike follow the Lake Trail over an old road that was once a carriage road to the Griffith Lake House, a clubhouse on the west side of Griffith Lake, then known as Buffum Pond, owned by Silas L. Griffith. The foundation of the house can still be seen. Silas Griffith, Vermont's first millionaire, lived in Danby and operated a sawmill camp, or job, that became known as the town of Griffith. That site is now called Old Job.

How to Get There

Drive 2.2 miles south of Danby on US 7, or 6.1 miles north of VT 7A, to South End Road. Turn left onto the road, and follow it east, crossing a set of railroad tracks. Pass a small cemetery on the right, and in 0.5 mile reach a small parking lot for five to six cars on the left.

The Trail

Your pathway starts at the right rear corner of the lot and ascends on easy grades. You soon cross a brook, hike parallel to the brook, and cross two smaller brooks, passing a lot of stinging nettles. At 0.75 mile the old roadway widens through a hemlock grove but quickly narrows and begins a sweeping switchback to your left, leaving the brook sounds behind. Pass a sign indicating the boundary of the Big Branch Wilderness Area at 0.9 mile, and continue climbing past a steep ledge on your right.

Imagine the labor required to construct the old road. At 1.6 miles you cross a rock slab on a narrow bridge. Through the trees

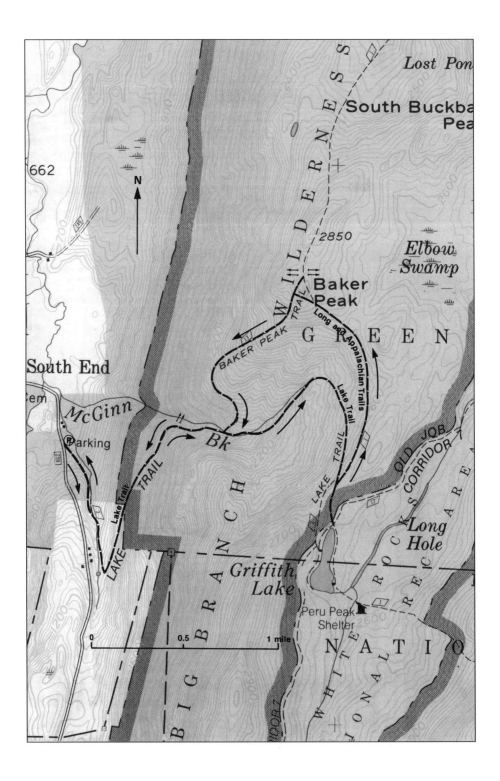

on the left, there are glimpses of Dorset Quarry across the valley. Look below in the rock for the metal pins that once held the carriage road bridge in place. A notch in the mountain ridge is visible ahead as the trail swings right. The trail gets steeper as you follow along McGinn Brook, on your left, flowing out of the valley. At 1.9 miles, cross McGinn Brook on rocks (this can be tricky when the water is high), and reach the junction with the Baker Peak Trail, on which you will return.

The Lake Trail bears right, continues upstream on easy grades, and crosses a brook as the trail becomes quite wet and rocky. Numerous small brooks cross the trail in this section. The trail bears right into the woods to avoid a very wet part of the old roadway. You soon return to the old road and pass through a maple forest on easy grades. The trail leaves the road at an obscure junction, crests a small knob, and reaches the Long Trail (LT)/Appalachian Trail (AT) junction at 3.3 miles.

Turn right, and follow the white-blazed LT/AT to Griffith Lake. A high, 16-acre mountain lake, Griffith Lake was originally called Buffum Pond. This warm-water lake averages 10 feet deep and, although stocked with brook trout, is not a particularly good fishing site. All camping at the lake is restricted to designated sites on the east shore, and a small fee is charged for overnight use. A Green Mountain Club caretaker is stationed at the lake during hiking season to assist hikers, maintain the local trails and shelters, and compost sewage at the tenting area and at Peru Peak Shelter, 0.5 mile south of the lake. A small camping fee is charged.

After enjoying the lake, return to the trail junction at 3.5 miles, and follow the LT/AT north along a relatively level grade to Baker Peak. From the junction, hike up, down, and over wet areas on puncheon until you reach a large boulder. Continue over several rock shelves with occasional views along the birch-lined hillside. At 5.4 miles, you reach the Baker Peak Trail Junction. Follow the LT/AT up the exposed rock slab to the summit. Be very careful of your footing along the slab. From the summit of Baker Peak, you have great views of Dorset Peak directly across the valley, Mount Equinox and the Stratton Mountain fire tower to the south, and the Otter Creek meandering through the narrow Valley of Vermont below.

From the summit, return to the junction, and steeply descend the ridge along the blue-blazed Baker Peak Trail. You quickly reach an overlook—called Quarry View—of the stone quarries on Dorset Peak. After enjoying the view, descend more gradually along a rock outcrop through mixed hardwoods. The trail soon bears right and begins a steep descent until you enter a fern-filled maple forest, where the trail levels slightly and resembles an old road. You begin to hear water as you reach the Lake Trail Junction at 6.9 miles. Turn right, cross the brook, and return along the old carriage road to your car at 8.2 miles.

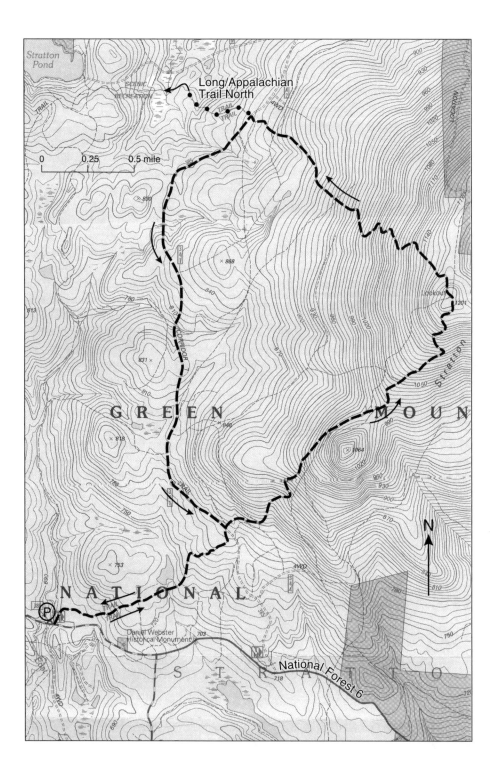

14

Stratton Mountain

Total distance: 9.3-mile loop

Hiking time: 6 hours

Vertical rise: 1,910 feet

Rating: Moderately strenuous

Map: USGS 7.5' Stratton Mountain

This long, beautiful loop hike visits a fire tower on the summit of Stratton Mountain. At 3,936 feet in elevation, it is the highest point in southern Vermont. The fire tower offers views that overlook Somerset Reservoir and Stratton Pond as well as the many mountains in southern Vermont and beyond. You can also hike to the fire tower and back on the same trail for a shorter trip of 7.6 miles. This out-and-back route up moderate grades to the mountaintop makes a fine, daylong snowshoe trip in winter.

Stratton Mountain played an important role in the conception of both the Long Trail (LT) and the Appalachian Trail (AT). On Stratton Mountain in 1909, James P. Taylor thought about a "long trail" that would link the summits of the Green Mountains. Several years later, on the same mountain, Benton MacKaye was inspired to develop an entire trail system along the Appalachian Mountains from Georgia to Maine.

How to Get There

Take VT 100 to the junction of Stratton-Arlington Road (or Kelley Stand Road) in West Wardsboro (0.0 mile). Drive 7.1 miles west on Stratton-Arlington Road to the LT/AT parking lot on the north side of the road. There is parking space for 8 to 10 cars. A U.S. Forest Service (USFS) sign marks the trailhead. In winter, the Stratton-Arlington Road is not plowed west of the trailhead.

The Trail

Begin your hike north along the white-blazed LT/AT up the bank behind the park-

Looking northwest from Stratton Mountain

ing area. You immediately cross a grassy logging road, enter the woods, and climb onto a small knob. Numerous old logging roads intersect the trail, and at times you follow them for a short distance while crossing several wet areas on puncheon. At 0.7 mile you pass below an old beaver dam, Behind the dam, the area originally covered by the beaver pond is quickly filling with trees and shrubs. Walk uphill through a mixed hard- and softwood forest, and at 1.1 miles, pass by an old farm site with apple trees, a stone wall, and several foundations. Hike through an overgrown pasture, and continue through a birch stand. Cross the gated, gravel USFS Road 341 (or International Paper IP Road) at 1.3 miles. Make a note of this junction, because you will be completing your return loop along this road.

Beyond the road, the trail crosses a small brook and passes by several old logging roads. The trail begins to ascend, gets steeper as it climbs over uneven rocks, and reaches a shelf at 1.7 miles with an overgrown view to the south; this is the col between Stratton Mountain and Little Stratton Mountain. Continue your ascent up the ridge through a mixed hardwood forest with numerous birches. At 2.5 miles, intersect the original route of the Stratton Mountain Trail.

In 1985, the Nature Conservancy acquired 12,000 acres of the western slope of Stratton Mountain, including the summit, and held it in trust until the USFS received the allocated money. In 1986, after years of negotiation with the property owner, International Paper Company, the USFS obtained funding to make the purchase final. The relocation of the LT/AT over Stratton Mountain, which involved 8.7 miles of new trail, was completed in 1989.

Continue your hike parallel to the ridgeline as the trail becomes nearly level. Climb again among higher-elevation spruce and birch, and come to another overgrown view at 2.75 miles of Somerset Reservoir and Mount Snow. Beyond the overlook, ascend past a spring on your left. You now hike through primarily balsam fir trees along several switchbacks until you reach the fire tower at 3.8 miles.

Stratton Mountain was one of the earliest fire-tower sites in Vermont. A steel tower was constructed in 1914. In the early 1930s, the Civilian Conservation Corps built a new cabin and a steel lookout tower. This tower, abandoned as a fire tower around 1980, was renovated by the USFS in 1988. It is one of two fire towers remaining on USFS Vermont lands and was nominated to the National Register of Historic Places in 1989.

A summit caretaker, supported by the Green Mountain Club, Appalachian Trail Conference, and Green Mountain National Forest, is stationed on the summit during the hiking season. No camping is permitted on the summit.

From the tower you can enjoy spectacular views: to the south, Somerset Reservoir and Mount Snow; to the southwest, Glastenbury Mountain; to the west, Mount Equinox and the Taconic Range; to the northeast, Mount Ascutney; and to the southeast, Mount Monadnock. Unless you decide to take the shorter 7.6-mile route back down the same trail to your car, continue north on the LT/AT along the summit ridge, and begin to descend. At 3.9 miles, you reach an overlook of Stratton Pond with Mount Equinox in the distance. In the next section, the trail uses stone steps, water bars, and turnpiking to cross a wet area.

At 4.4 miles you steeply descend over rocks and roots in the trail and begin a series of long switchbacks through a softwood forest. As the trail passes through mixed hardwoods, continue your descent, and cross a brook at 5.1 miles. The trail soon intersects several old logging roads, descends for a short distance, and crosses a wet area on puncheon.

After a more moderate descent, you reach the gravel IP Road at 5.8 miles. The LT/AT goes 1 mile straight ahead to Stratton Pond. Turn left, and follow the rough gravel road south to the LT/AT intersection (at 8.3 miles), which you passed earlier in your hike. Turn right, and follow the LT/AT south back down the trail to your car at 9.3 miles.

15

Little Rock Pond and Clarendon Gorge

Total distance: 15.0 miles

Hiking time: 2 days, 1 night

Vertical rise: 3,100 feet

Rating: Day 1–moderate; Day 2–easy

Maps: USGS 7.5' Wallingford; 7.5' Rutland

This enjoyable hike along the Long Trail/ Appalachian Trail (LT/AT) is appropriate for even a novice backpacker. The trail crosses valleys, passes mountain ponds, follows ridgelines, crests mountains, and concludes across a suspension bridge over Clarendon Gorge. There are ample opportunities both days for swimming as well as numerous scenic vistas.

The suspension bridge over the gorge was built in 1974. For several years, until the mid-1950s, an old timber bridge spanned the gorge, but it was removed when it decayed and became unsafe. The Green Mountain Club's Killington Section planned a new bridge in 1955 and completed construction in the spring of 1957. The bridge held strong until the flood of 1973 washed it away. Four days later, tragedy struck when 17-year-old Robert Brugmann, attempting to cross the still-swollen river on a fallen tree, slipped, fell into the stream, and drowned.

A subsequent relocation made such a long detour to reach the bridge in East Clarendon that the GMC planned a new bridge. With a design from GMC member Allan St. Peter, major technical assistance from the Vermont Department of Highways, and memorial gifts from Robert Brugmann's family and friends, construction started in the spring of 1974. The bridge cost almost $8,000, quite a difference from the $700 bridge constructed in 1957! Highway engineers, U.S. Forest Service (USFS) personnel, and GMC volunteers worked together to complete the bridge in July 1974.

The first day, you hike past Little Rock Pond and over White Rocks Mountain to Greenwall Shelter, where you spend the night. Little Rock Pond is one of the most popular day-use and overnight-use areas on the LT. The pond is a good fishing spot and is annually stocked with brook trout. Beavers frequent the area, and moose have occasionally been sighted along the pond shore. Careful management is required to preserve the area's natural beauty and fragile shoreline environment. Because of the area's high use, a GMC caretaker is stationed at the site during the hiking season. An overnight-use fee is charged.

The second day, you cross VT 140, traverse Bear Mountain, hike through overgrown farmlands and pastures, continue along a rocky ridge, and finish by crossing the suspension bridge at Clarendon Gorge.

How to Get There

Spot a car on the south side of VT 103 at the Clarendon Gorge parking area, 2.1 miles east of US 7, approximately 5.0 miles south of Rutland. Avoid the temptation to explore the gorge so that it remains the reward at the end of your journey. Vandalism can be a problem at this parking area; see the introduction for specific precautions to follow.

To reach the trail where you begin your journey, take US 7 south to Danby, where a sign points east to Mount Tabor and USFS Road 10. Turn east (left) onto USFS Road 10, and drive 3.5 miles to the Long Trail Parking Area at Big Black Branch. Because this trailhead is popular with hikers traveling to Little Rock Pond, there is an outhouse as well as a trailhead information board.

The Trail

Day One
Total distance: 7.0 miles
Hiking time: 4½ hours
Vertical rise: 1,275 feet

Begin your hike over easy terrain along the Little Black Branch on an old road. At 0.6 mile, cross the brook on a single I-beam bridge, and bear right along the brook. Notice that the brook gets smaller as you cross it again. Continue up the hillside, occasionally on puncheon. At 1.8 miles, you reach a spur on the right to Lula Tye Shelter, which was moved from Little Rock Pond's east shore to this location in 1972 to reduce hiker impact on the pond area. The shelter is named in memory of the GMC's corresponding secretary from 1926 to 1955.

Continue on the LT/AT on a rocky path until you approach the end of Little Rock Pond, where a signboard explains the pond ecology and area trails. Bear right, and come to a tenting area on a knoll behind the tent of the GMC caretaker, who is stationed at the site during the hiking season. Nestled among the mountains at an elevation of 1,854 feet, Little Rock Pond is a scenic place to swim, rest, and cool off. An overnight-use fee is charged.

Hike along the stony shore among dense conifers to the pond outlet at 2.4 miles, where the Green Mountain Trail bears left. Continue straight ahead and descend away from the pond to a spur on the right to Little Rock Pond Shelter. Built by the USFS in 1962, the shelter was moved in 1972 from its former location on the pond's small island.

From the shelter, the LT/AT passes through an old clearing on easy grades; this is the site of an abandoned lumber town,

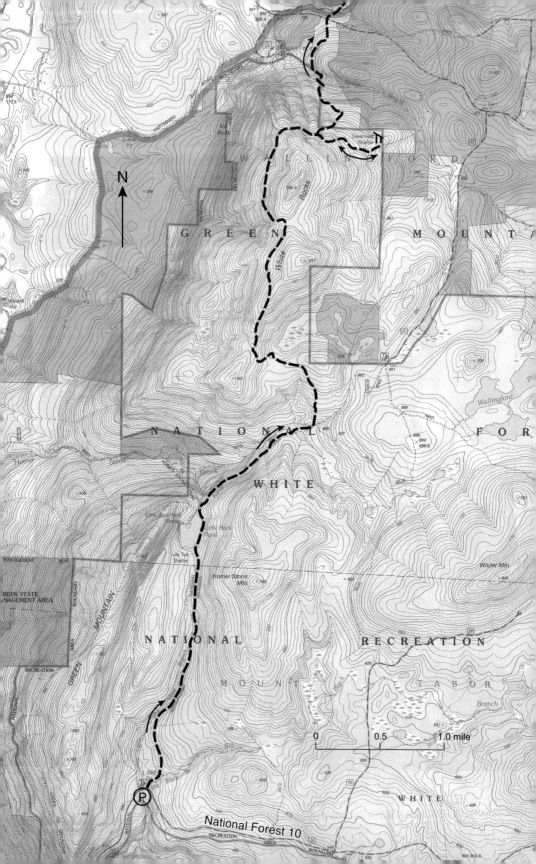

National Forest 10

The north shore of Little Rock Pond

Aldrichville. The USFS has been working with local high school students to excavate artifacts and has put up an interpretive sign along the trail near an old stone foundation. Soon cross Homer Stone Brook bridge and the old South Wallingford/Wallingford Pond Road at 3.3 miles. You now begin a steady and sometimes rocky ascent up White Rocks Mountain through dense red spruce and pass just west of the summit at 5.6 miles. An blue-blazed spur on the left leads downhill to a fantastic view from the top of White Rocks Cliff.

Descend to the Greenwall Spur junction at 6.8 miles. Follow the spur downhill to Greenwall Shelter, where you end your day at 7.0 miles. The shelter, a frame lean-to for eight, was built by the USFS in 1962. There are a few tenting sites behind the shelter. A blue-blazed trail leads 600 feet northeast to a spring, which may fail in very dry weather.

Day Two

Total distance: 8.0 miles
Hiking time: 5 hours
Vertical rise: 1,825 feet

Pack up and return up the spur to the LT/AT on the slope of White Rocks Mountain. Proceed north, descend to an old road, and follow it downhill to a junction with the Keewaydin Trail at 0.9 mile. Turn right, and cross Bully Brook, which you then follow downhill before bearing right to slab the slope through a shady hemlock grove. Continue your descent to gravel Sugar Hill Road at 1.6 miles, and then drop steeply down rock stairs to cross the Roaring Brook bridge, built by GMC's Volunteer Long Trail Patrol. Cross VT 140 carefully at 1.7 miles, and climb gently to the trailhead parking lot.

Cross the parking lot, and ascend the old road to an old pasture. Turn right to enter the pasture, and continue uphill through open forest, passing an old foundation, before turning right to join another abandoned road at 2.3 miles. Turn left to leave the road, and begin to climb Bear Mountain on switchbacks. A spur to the left leads to a great view south down the Valley of Vermont, flanked by White Rocks Mountain to the east and Dorset Peak to the west. Continue uphill, join an old road to ascend steeply through an oak forest, and reach the height-of-land just west of the main ridge of Bear Mountain, avoiding the power line to the airport beacon. Follow gentle grades to parallel the ridge, and then descend to a clearing—the north end of a beaver meadow—at 4.4 miles.

Descend on an old road that is also used locally as a cross-country ski trail, cross a power line, and join a gravel road briefly before bearing left uphill to a spur to your right leading to Minerva Hinchey Shelter at 5.3 miles. This three-sided frame structure is named for the GMC's corresponding secretary for 22 years from (1955–77). The shelter is a nice spot to eat lunch and rest before the final leg of your journey.

Continue your hike on the LT up a hard-wood ridge and down to Spring Lake Clearing. The USFS periodically clears this meadow in the spring through prescribed burns. By burning at appropriate and safe times, the growth of berry bushes, like raspberries and blackberries, is encouraged, whereas brush and trees are discouraged. This clearing is an effort to maintain the view and foster wildlife habitat.

Hike along the ridge until you reach Airport Lookout at 7.2 miles, with a good western view of the Otter Creek Valley, Rutland, and the Taconic Range. Descend steeply from the outcrop to Mill River and Clarendon Gorge at 7.9 miles. Cross the suspension bridge over the gorge. As you look down into the deep gorge, picture the river during floods, when the water can rise high enough to nearly touch the bridge! Ascend to the parking lot at 8.0 miles to complete your hike. After dropping off your gear at your car, you may wish to further explore and enjoy this scenic area and popular swimming hole.

On top of Mount Horrid's Great Cliff

DAVE HARDY

16

Robert Frost Trail

Total distance: 1-mile loop

Hiking time: ¾ hour

Vertical rise: 120 feet

Rating: Easy

Map: USGS 7.5' East Middlebury

Robert Frost (1874–1936) spent 23 summers in a small cabin in the Ripton area. He considered himself a Vermonter by preference and was considered by his community to be Ripton's First Citizen. Frost located here seasonally because of his involvement with the Middlebury School of English and its writer's conference. This trail, constructed in 1976 by the Youth Conservation Corps, commemorates his poetry in a location near his summer residence. Prepare yourself; this may be the most poetic hike you'll ever take—literally. Many of Frost's best-loved poems, and some not so well known, are mounted on plaques along the loop trail. Walkers will also find many signs that label features of the natural environment. Visitors may also wish to stop at the Robert Frost Wayside Recreation Area, with picnic tables and information boards, 0.2 mile east of the trailhead on VT 125.

How to Get There

The trail is located on VT 125, 2.1 miles east of Ripton (itself 2 miles east of VT 116), or 9.8 miles west of VT 100 in Hancock. There is a U.S. Forest Service trailhead parking area for 10 to 20 cars. A trail map signboard at the parking area shows the location of the trail system and lists significant dates and facts about Robert Frost. A handicapped-accessible trail loop is included at the beginning of the trail system, and a modern privy is also located at the trailhead.

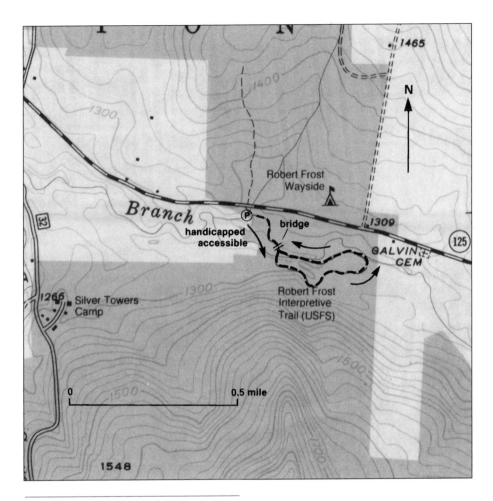

The Trail

The walk described below is essentially a figure-8. Although a sign located just to the right of the signboard indicates that the trail starts to your right, instead bear left, following the gravel, handicapped-accessible path past thick meadow growth. You will arrive at a junction where Frost's poem, "Stopping by a Woods on a Snowy Evening," is posted. Turn left here, and just ahead cross a bridge over the South Branch of the Middlebury River. After the bridge, turn right, and ascend to a grove of red spruce overlooking the river. You will

begin to notice that the trail is now occasionally marked with blue markers. Just ahead, the trail arrives at a junction with another trail. Keep left here, as the trail you are on swings to the left through hay-scented ferns and continues following an easy grade through the forest. Signs identify many of the trees and plants along the way.

At 0.5 mile, pass through a birch grove, and then enter an open meadow. A sign here provides profiles of the area mountains, including Firetower Hill, Bread Loaf Mountain, Battell Mountain, Kirby Mountain, and Burnt Hill. The trail swings left through the meadow and comes to a bench over-looking the river. Frost's poem, "Going for Water," is posted here.

The trail now parallels the river cutting through thick field growth. Prescribed burning is used to keep the meadow open and encourage the growth of blueberries and huckleberries. Leaving this open environ-ment, the trail re-enters the woods, and then returns to the bridge you crossed earlier. At the first junction ("Stopping by Woods..."), keep left, passing through a large black-berry patch. The trail now rises onto a large wooden boardwalk that leads over a swamp and then swings to the right, arriving back at the trailhead at 1.0 mile.

17

Texas Falls

Total distance: 1.2-mile loop

Hiking time: ¾ hour

Vertical rise: 160 feet

Rating: Easy

Map: USGS 7.5' Bread Loaf

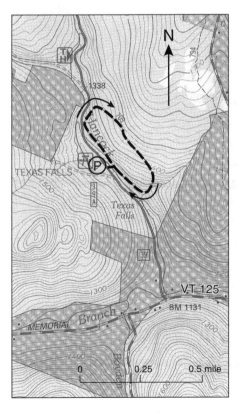

Impressive waterfalls and geological formations make this interpretive trail an enjoyable, easy hike through part of the Green Mountain National Forest. Texas Brook, part of a watershed that drains this 9-square-mile area east of the main ridge of the Green Mountains, begins approximately 3 miles to the north as a seasonal stream, then makes its way to Hancock Branch, the White River, the Connecticut River, and, finally, the Atlantic Ocean.

How to Get There

Drive west on VT 125 from the intersection with VT 100 in Hancock (0.0 mile) to the signpost for GMNF TEXAS FALLS RECREATION AREA at 3.0 miles. Turn right, and follow Texas Falls Road north to a small parking area on your left at 3.5 miles. Additional parking is available at a picnic area up the road at 3.75 miles.

The Trail

The trail begins opposite the parking area, where you see and hear Texas Falls. Elaborate stone steps and walls descend to the falls and provide breathtaking views into the deep ravine.

Cross the bridge over Texas Brook, turn left, and ascend upstream on more steps. You soon reach a registration box, which provides interpretive pamphlets for two interconnecting nature trails. The first trail follows the stream for 0.3 mile, then takes the road back to the parking area. The second trail continues along an upper trail 0.75 mile in a loop back to the falls. Benches along

Texas Falls

the way allow you to linger, read the guide, and enjoy the trail.

As you walk upstream, still in sight of the brook and road, note the exposed roots and rocks along the trail. People walking off the trail and compacting the ground so that the roots are unable to penetrate the hard soil cause this erosion. Please help stop further erosion by staying on the trail.

As you continue your hike through the evergreen forest, be sure to enjoy the fragrant air. The pamphlet explains that evergreens are "ever green" because their leaves are more efficient than those of deciduous trees at retaining life-sustaining water during the winter. Adaptations include a smaller surface area, a waxy coating, and resin that protects them from freezing.

As you gently climb along the wide, gravel trail, be sure to look for old aspen trees and lichens that appear on boulders. Also, take time to rest on one of several benches. The trail continues along a fern-covered bank to the crest of a hill. Hike down the hill, look for a bridge, and read the plywood disk designed to help you identify area trees. At 0.3 mile, drop off your pamphlet at the registration box, and descend to the road and your car, or continue along the upper trail.

To continue your hike, turn right, and climb along an old logging road that is also used for winter snowmobiling. The trail soon takes a sharp right and climbs to the top of the next rise as you pass through a stand of mixed hard- and softwood trees. At 0.6 mile, you cross two small brooks and then descend to a hemlock stand. Continue downhill to the falls and over a bridge. After a few steps and switchbacks, follow the loop trail down into the gorge. A side trail to your left descends to a lookout. At 1.1 miles, return the pamphlet to the registration box, cross the brook, marvel again at the beautiful falls, and continue to the renovated picnic area for lunch at 1.2 miles.

18

Quechee Gorge

Total distance: 1.6 miles

Hiking time: 1 hour

Vertical rise: 250 feet

Rating: Easy

Map: USGS 7.5' Quechee

Quechee Gorge is a popular tourist attraction in summer and provides Nordic ski opportunities in winter. It is suitable for families with children because a 4-foot steel chain-link fence prevents falling into the 170-foot deep gorge. This easy hike features spectacular views of the Quechee Gorge and the Ottauquechee River, which traverses it. The name Ottauquechee came from the Native American word meaning "swift mountain stream."

Quechee Gorge was formed approximately 13,000 years ago, toward the end of the last glacial age. About 6,000 years before that, the climate warmed significantly, and the most recent glacier began to recede. A natural dam of debris, rocks, sand, and gravel—a glacial moraine—was deposited in what is now Connecticut. This created a narrow lake, Lake Hitchcock, up the Connecticut River Valley from Rocky Hill, Connecticut, to northern Vermont. Water and ice were also impounded in the valleys of tributaries to the Connecticut River, including the Ottauquechee River, which flows through the Quechee Gorge. When the dam broke about 13,000 years ago, Lake Hitchcock was drained, and the water in the Ottauquechee Valley rushed downstream carrying a torrent of sand, clay, gravel, and rocks, which cut the gorge into the bedrock. The scouring of the bedrock continues to this time.

How to Get There

Leave I-89 at exit 1, and drive west on US 4 to Deweys Mills Road on your right just be-

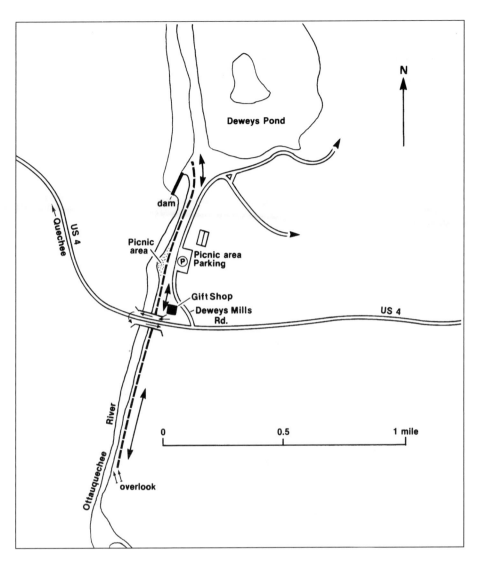

fore the Quechee Gorge bridge. This road is 2.5 miles from the southbound exit ramp and 3.2 miles from the northbound ramp. The large paved parking area fronts on US 4, extends on both sides of Deweys Mills Road, and is associated with a small mall.

The Trail

The trailhead is located at the west end of the parking lot, near the Quechee Gorge

Gift Shop. Turn right, and walk 0.3 mile north to a dam, hydroelectic power station, and Deweys Mills Pond. The dam was once the location of the Dewey Woolen Mill. Retrace your steps over crushed stone back to the bridge.

The gorge was once a popular resort. The river was very difficult to cross. Early bridges over the river often collapsed or were swept away by the current. The original bridge spanning the gorge was a railway bridge built in 1875 for the Woodstock Railroad. Historian William Tucker reported that "nearly 3,000 people assembled to celebrate the long anticipated event." The present steel arch was built for the railroad in 1911. In 1933, the tracks were removed and replaced with the roadbed of US 4.

After returning to the trailhead, continue walking south 0.5 mile. The trail descends into the gorge to the bedrock, where you can see the grooved, broken rock left over the centuries by water, sand, clay, and rocks. Backtrack to the trailhead, and walk up on the bridge, which has protected walkways on both sides of the road. Enjoy the views of the gorge before returning to your car.

19

Mount Horrid's Great Cliff

Total distance: 1.4 miles

Hiking time: 1 hour

Vertical rise: 620 feet

Rating: Moderate

Map: USGS 7.5' Mount Carmel

This short steep hike takes you to the top of the Great Cliff. According to a Green Mountain National Forest sign:

> The rock that makes up the exposed face of this cliff was formed during earliest geological times. Freezing and thawing have wedged off fragments which have accumulated over time on the mountain slope.

Be aware that the trail may be closed when peregrine falcons are nesting on the cliff overlook. Before they were reintroduced by the state into the area, falcons had not nested on these cliffs for 50 years. A nesting pair released several years ago has returned to the area. Peregrine falcons are extremely sensitive to human disturbance, especially from above, and may abandon their nest if approached too closely. Please obey all posted trail signs during nesting season, and see the introduction for more information on the falcons. In recent years, the falcons have been nesting at the far eastern end of the cliffs, so closing the cliff overlook hasn't been necessary.

How to Get There

Follow VT 73 to the top of Brandon Gap. Just west of the gap summit, there is a large parking lot on the south side of the road. Before parking your car, however, stop at the pull-off area just east of the gap summit for a view of the cliffs and a beaver pond as well as information boards describing the cliffs and pond ecology. After enjoying the views, return to the parking lot at the top of the gap.

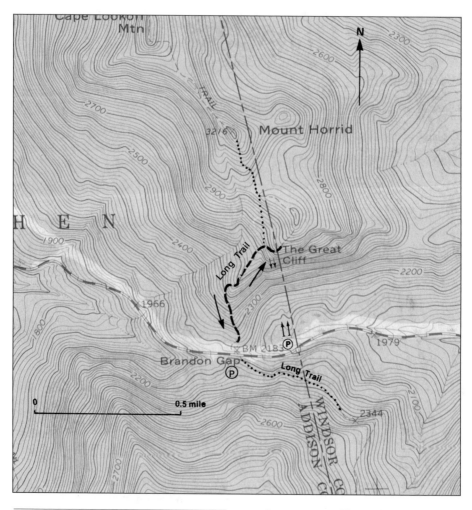

The Trail

Carefully cross VT 73, climb the embankment on an old road, and begin hiking north on the white-blazed Long Trail (LT). You cross a small raspberry patch and ascend to a Green Mountain National Forest registration box and sign that indicates a distance of 0.6 mile to the Great Cliff overlook.

After the sign, the trail steeply ascends on log steps to a ridge at 0.2 mile. Birches line the trail along the ridge until you ascend more steps. The trail swings to the western side of the ridge, passes through mixed hardwoods, and becomes much rockier and steeper. When climbing steeply over rock steps that may be slippery if conditions are wet, watch your step, and stay on the trail to limit erosion in this area. Through the trees to your right, the Great Cliff looms above you. Climb an extensive staircase, built by U.S. Forest Service and Green Mountain Club trail crews, and at the top of the stairs reach a trail junction at 0.6 mile. To the left, the LT continues north to the sum-

Mount Horrid's cliff

mit of Mount Horrid, and to the right, a blue-blazed spur leads uphill 500 feet to the cliff overlook. As you step out into the opening, you are on top of the 2,800-foot Mount Horrid Overlook seen from the parking area—now 700 feet below. Also below is the beaver pond you saw from the pull-off.

After enjoying the views, including Bloodroot Gap to the south, hike back down the same trail to Brandon Gap. The descent is easier, but watch your footing, especially on steep sections in wet conditions.

Mount Horrid's Great Cliff

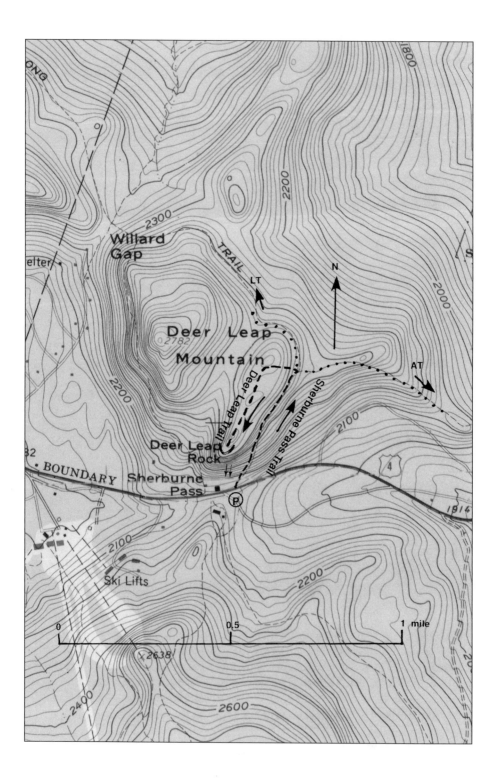

20

Deer Leap Overlook

Total distance: 2 miles

Hiking time: 1¼ hours

Vertical rise: 520 feet

Rating: Easy

Map: USGS 7.5' Pico Peak

The Deer Leap Trail is a unique introductory day hike that includes portions of the former Long Trail (LT) and Appalachian Trail (AT), as well as a side trail that leads to a spectacular view from the top of Deer Leap Cliffs. The cliffs are a popular climbing area, so be sure to look for rock climbers.

In southern Vermont, the AT coincides with the LT from the Massachusetts border to Maine Junction in Willard Gap, a mile north of where both trails cross US 4. From there the AT continues east through Vermont and across the White Mountains in New Hampshire to Maine. The LT heads north to Canada.

Built by volunteers between 1921 and 1937, the AT extends 2,100 miles from Springer Mountain in Georgia to Mount Katahdin in Maine. Benton MacKaye, a forester, author, and philosopher, first proposed it in 1921. On Stratton Mountain in Vermont, MacKaye conceived the idea of connecting the high peaks of the East after construction of the LT had already begun. Today, nearly 30 local nonprofit trail groups, such as the Green Mountain Club; individual volunteers; community groups; and more than 80 local, state, and federal agencies in 14 states (all coordinated through the Appalachian Trail Conference) maintain, manage, and preserve this valuable recreational resource.

How to Get There

Take US 4 to the top of Sherburne Pass, 9.1 miles east of US 7 in Rutland. Park in the lot opposite the Inn at Long Trail on the

Pico Peak from Deer Leap Overlook

south side of the highway, where there is ample parking.

The Trail

Carefully cross US 4, where traffic travels at high speeds, and begin your hike on the north side of US 4 to the east (right) of the inn. Follow the blue-blazed Sherburne Pass Trail over the first set of boulders. Be careful to avoid the old Deer Leap Lookout Trail on your left, which has been closed and relocated because of severe erosion, Native American cultural concerns, and hazardous footing. You soon pass over more boulders.

They provide the roughest footing of the hike, but also make some interesting little caves where they are jumbled. The trail descends to your right to avoid a steep rock face, levels out, and then ascends until you reach a trail junction at 0.5 mile. Be sure not to take a right turn, which would take you on the AT (blazed in white) to Maine. This was Maine Junction from 1966 until 1999, when the LT/AT north of Pico Peak was moved west to avoid possible ski area expansion and the former LT/AT became the Sherburne Pass Trail. (Before 1966, Maine Junction was at Sherburne Pass, and the LT went west around Deer Leap Mountain on its way to Canada.)

Continue straight ahead "southbound" toward Georgia (actually heading north here) on the white-blazed AT, and in 200 feet reach the junction of the blue-blazed Deer Leap Trail. The U.S. Forest Service constructed this trail in 1994 to replace the eroded and unsafe Deer Leap Lookout Trail.

Turn left onto the Deer Leap Trail, and ascend mostly through white birches until you crest a series of small spruce- and fir-covered knobs beginning at 0.8 mile. Look for the trail sign at the junction of the Overlook Spur near a boulder on your right at 0.9 mile, just beyond the 2,585-foot west summit of Little Deer Leap. (To the right, the Deer Leap Trail continues over Big Deer Leap and reaches the AT in another mile, 0.7 mile from where you left it.) Keep left at this junction to remain on the Overlook Spur, and continue along the spruce- and fir-lined ridge of Little Deer Leap until it opens onto a small, but long rock shelf. Keeping to the left side, descend the shelf face. Just beyond the shelf, the trail opens onto the Deer Leap Cliffs at 1.0 mile. The rocks can be slippery, and the overlook is quite steep, so use caution.

Enjoy the views of Pico Peak directly across Sherburne Pass and the sweeping views to the east and west. The remains of the old Long Trail Lodge are in the woods just south of US 4 and west of the parking lot. You may also see some technical rock climbers, as this is a popular rock-climbing area. After resting and enjoying the views, return to your car along the same trails, exercising caution that you keep to the south and west back to Sherburne Pass.

21

Mount Independence

Total distance: 2.5 miles

Hiking time: 1½ hours

Vertical rise: 200 feet

Rating: Easy to moderate

Map: USGS 7.5' Ticonderoga

Mount Independence was Vermont's major Revolutionary War fortification and is one of the least disturbed Revolutionary War sites in the United States. With its north-facing orientation, steep cliffs, and 300-foot elevation above Lake Champlain, it was an important strategic defense component against a British attack from Canada.

When American General Philip Schuyler ordered troops to begin clearing land on what was then Rattlesnake Hill or East Point in 1776, his plan was to prevent the British fleet from sailing down Lake Champlain and dividing New England from the rest of the colonies. Later that summer, on July 28, after a reading of the Declaration of Independence, the soldiers renamed their fortification Mount Independence. In October, General Guy Carleton, fresh from his victory over Benedict Arnold and the fledgling American fleet at Valcour Island, sailed south toward Mount Independence and Fort Ticonderoga. Arnold's fleet bought the time necessary to upgrade the fortifications; Carleton was so impressed with the two fortifications and the twelve to thirteen thousand troops stationed there that he turned north, retreating to Canada before the onset of winter, thus delaying the British invasion for another year. Twenty-five hundred troops spent a hard winter on the mount with seven or eight soldiers freezing to death each night.

In the summer of 1777, the British returned, and the Americans, under the command of General Arthur St. Clair, retreated southward with the enemy close at their heels. British General John "Gentleman Johnny" Bourgoyne left troops to guard the fort. After the British defeat at Saratoga, these soldiers burned most of Mount Independence's buildings and hightailed it back to Canada. After the war, Mount Independence was used to pasture livestock, its significance largely forgotten.

In 1912, Sarah Pell purchased the northern half of Mount Independence and began working to preserve the site. Her son, John, deeded the land to the Fort Ticonderoga Association in 1952–53. The state of Vermont purchased an additional 108 acres in 1961 and 1973, and these two institutions manage the site today. Mount Independence is open from Memorial Day to Labor Day. The worthwhile visitors center, built in 1996, houses exhibits, artifacts, and an informational video. Site maps and guided tours are available. There is an entry fee.

How to Get There

Mount Independence lies 6 miles west of the junction of VT 22A and VT 73 in Orwell. From VT 22A, turn west onto VT 73. At 0.3 mile, bear left at a road junction, avoiding a side road on your left. At 4.8 miles, the paved road turns to gravel. At 5.2 miles, you come to the junction with Catfish Bay Road. Turn left, up the steep narrow road. The bateau-shaped visitors center is on your right (5.3 miles), and parking is across the road on your left.

The Trail

From the visitors center, follow a crushed stone path uphill to a signboard. Continue up the hill, following the remnants of an old road to a kiosk. Turn left from the kiosk, and follow the blue- and red-blazed trail on a mown path into the woods to the site of the former field hospital, sheltered by a small stand of white pines. Standing in this

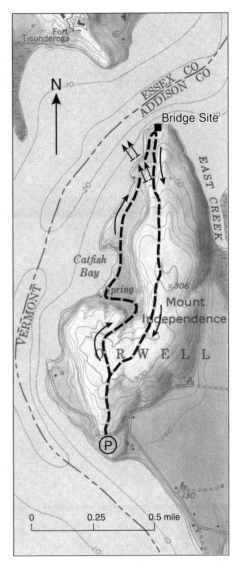

peaceful spot, it's hard to imagine the suffering that took place in the winter of 1776–77. Here, the red and blue trails split, and the blue trail begins a long descent on a moderate grade. You will cross a small footbridge at the bottom of the hill and continue on a long level stretch, catching glimpses of Catfish Bay on your left. This area may be muddy in spring. After coming

Mount Independence

M.L. RECOR

to an open meadow—the garden area—the trail turns right and re-enters the woods. Immediately on your right is what is believed to have been the original water source for the fort. The trail now becomes a pleasant woods walk to a grassy meadow with a view directly across the lake to Mount Defiance, from which British soldiers monitored activity inside the picket fort on Mount Independence.

The trail switchbacks right into the woods, passing a former French stone quarry on the right. The French hauled stone from this spot across the ice to build Fort Carillon, now known as Ticonderoga. The blue trail soon ends at a junction with the orange trail, marked with a sign. Continue straight on the orange-blazed trail, down a small hill to the masting point on your left. The view from here is worth the short scramble to the high point. The cliffs drop precipitously to the water below, and it is thought masts were lowered from the top

into the hulls of newly built ships. At the next junction, where the orange trail forks, bear left down to the shore and site of the floating bridge. In the winter of 1776–77, American troops stationed at Mount Independence built log cribs on the ice, sinking them in the spring. These became the foundation for a floating bridge across the narrows to Fort Ticonderoga. In his journal, British Lieutenant Digby described the American effort: "The enemy, with their usual industry, had joined these two posts by a bridge of communication thrown over the inlet. This was like many of their performances, a great and most laborious work."

Either retrace your steps to the last junction and take the right fork, now on your left, or walk north 50 feet along the flat rock to a path leading steeply away from the lake. Both routes lead to a prominent obelisk erected by the Hand's Cove Chapter of the Daughters of the American Revolution in

1908 to commemorate the soldiers buried on Mount Independence (1775–84).

Continuing north through the clearing, past the monument, you pass a signboard and reenter the woods on the orange trail. Soon you reach a junction; the trail on the right leads back to the blue trail. Bear left on the orange trail, marked with a RETURN TRAIL sign, and continue to a second junction. Both of these orange-blazed trails return to the visitors center, but the one on the right is the more scenic. Taking the right fork, you come to a spur trail leaving right a short distance to the remains of the horseshoe battery and a monument erected by the National Society of the Colonial Dames of America. From here, you have the best view across to Fort Ticonderoga.

Return to the main trail, and begin a gradual ascent to an open meadow, one-time site of artisans' shops. Walking over 25 feet of log corduroy and entering the woods, you come to a second spur, which leads to the site of the crane used to hoist cargo from ships floating down below to the fort on the hill above. The orange trail bears left, marked with an arrow, and continues up a slight grade to the highest point on Mount Independence, Barracks Square. Cedar trees planted around the perimeter mark the outline of the Star Fort. The trail turns right, and two orange-blazed trails leave the clearing. Either will return you to the kiosk and visitors center.

22

Mount Tom

Total distance: 3.5 miles

Hiking time: 2¼ hours

Vertical rise: 600 feet

Rating: Moderate

Maps: USGS 7.5' Woodstock North; 7.5' Woodstock South

Marsh–Billings–Rockefeller National Historic Park in Woodstock is Vermont's second national park; the Appalachian National Scenic Trail is its first. The estate was donated by the Rockefeller family and features historic buildings, a carefully managed forest landscape, and plenty of opportunities for walking and exploring the grounds. Mount Tom is but one of many wild destinations close to the heart of Woodstock. If time permits, the Billings Farm museum is well worth the visit. The trail system is operated as a cross-country ski touring center, with a fee, in winter.

How to Get There

From US 4 in Woodstock, follow VT 12 north 0.5 mile to the parking lot for Marsh–Billings–Rockefeller National Historic Park and Billings Farm Museum on your right.

The Trail

Cross the road using the crosswalk between the Farm Museum and the Marsh–Billings–Rockefeller Park. Start up the hill on the path. If you want to pick up the park service map of the carriage roads and all the trails through the park, at the fork take the left fork to the Carriage Barn, which serves as the park's visitors center (the carriage road is well signed, the trails in the historical park are unmarked). If you want to develop your own variations of hikes in this area, this is a useful map. There are also rest rooms, an interesting exhibit on the history of the park and on land stewardship, a small library, and the park ranger at the in-

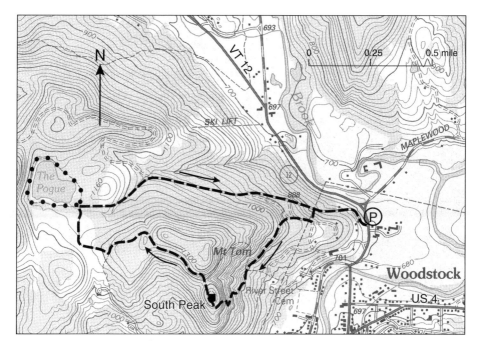

formation desk. If you visit the Carriage Barn, return to this fork to start the hike.

To begin the hike, at the fork bear right toward CARRIAGE ROAD AND TRAILS. Follow this wide dirt carriage road around the gate, passing a large, fancy woodshed on the right as you climb gently but steadily. Spring hikers should look for the wild ginger, jack-in-the-pulpit, and trillium. Take the first sharp left turn onto another wide carriage road, again going gently uphill. Reach a T-intersection, and turn right onto a wide carriage road near the horse shed's clearing. At the next T-intersection, turn right again onto a wide carriage road that leads away from the clearing. Take the first left onto a wide but less-worn carriage road that goes uphill and curves off to the left. Reach a T-intersection, and go right uphill. This road will rapidly diminish into a narrow trail. There are no signs or trail markings in this area, which is in the historical park. You will be walking through mixed hardwoods and evergreens of varying

ages, up to 80 to 100 years old. The trail contours across the south side of Mount Tom. You will start to see yellow blazes as you come around from the east to the southeast side of Mount Tom and pass into the town of Woodstock's Billings Park; all the trails within the town park are marked with yellow paint.

After a short walk, you start to trend upward, with some fine rock faces covered in thick moss and lichen on your right. You will reach trail signs that indicate that you've been on the Lower North Peak Trail. This sign is actually behind you and is more obvious to hikers walking in the opposite direction. In front of you will be a sign for Precipice Trail. Take the left fork, which goes downhill slightly by two switchbacks to cross a narrow small stream on rocks. Again, there are many beautiful rocks covered in thick moss and lichens. After crossing the stream, climb up moderately about 30 feet, and reach a bench and the junction

A pasture vista near The Pogue

DAVE HARDY

with the Upper Link Trail. Go straight on this trail (left will take you downhill into the town of Woodstock's Faulkner Park and out to Mountain Avenue), continuing to circle Mount Tom on a level trail. Look for lots more jack-in-the-pulpit, as well as jewelweed, wild parsley, and blue cohosh. Pass another bench and a sign that says PRECIPICE TRAIL (although you are actually on the Upper Link Trail). At the T-intersection 10 feet ahead, there is sign behind you that says LOWER LINK TRAIL and a sign ahead that says TO FAULKNER TRAIL.

Turn right, and go gently uphill. Cross a wet area on rocks, noting the rock jumble on the right. Continue trending around the mountain as you begin very gently going uphill. The woods change from tall hardwoods to tall evergreens. Pass two green railing posts on the right, and reach the junction of the Link Trail and the Faulkner Trail. Bear right slightly uphill (left will again take you downhill to Faulkner Park and Mountain Avenue).

The trail now ascends Mount Tom in long, very gentle switchbacks with many benches; views of Woodstock that can be caught through the trees, especially when the leaves are off; occasional remains of fencing; a short, low-rising rock staircase; and an alternation of types of trees, with a large number of oak trees. You will come to an area with two split log benches together and a sign that says SUMMIT 100 YARDS. There is a good view here looking east into New Hampshire and southeast through the trees to Mount Ascutney.

The trail takes a short dip, and then climbs moderately uphill, with some rock steps and some wire handrails to the top. Here you meet the carriage road on the top of the south peak of Mount Tom. There are several benches, with views to the east into New Hampshire, southeast to Mount Ascutney, and south to Woodstock in the valley (note the town green and the Woodstock Inn). There is also a huge pair of wooden posts with lights in a star that is visible in Woodstock.

Turn left onto the carriage road, and follow it about a half-mile to a crossroad. Turn left at a sign, THE POGUE 0.1. When you reach the Pogue you can add 0.75 mile to your hike by circling this man-made pond on a carriage road. To return to the visitors center from here via carriage road, just follow the signs east for the visitors center.

23

Rattlesnake Point

Total distance: 3.9 miles

Hiking time: 2½ hours

Vertical rise: 1,160 feet

Rating: Moderate

Map: USGS 7.5' East Middlebury

Rattlesnake Point, a large rock outcrop at the southern end of Mount Moosalamoo, provides spectacular views of two lakes and the regions beyond. This trail, which begins on Green Mountain National Forest land, was completed in 1977 by the Youth Conservation Corps and rebuilt in 1983 by a crew from the Rutland Community Correctional Center. This blue-blazed U.S. Forest Service (USFS) trail begins a loop that links the Falls of Lana Picnic Area, Rattlesnake Point, Mount Moosalamoo, and the Moosalamoo Campground. Hikers should be warned that peregrine falcons are known to nest on the steep cliffs. When they do, the Forest Service will close the trail to the cliffs, usually from April to August. Hikers may wish to call the USFS (Middlebury Ranger District) ahead of time if planning to hike during this period.

How to Get There

The trail is located on VT 53, 5.7 miles north of VT 73 in Forest Dale or 4.1 miles south of US 7 near Middlebury. A USFS sign indicating Silver Lake and Falls of Lana designate the parking area.

The Trail

The trailhead is located behind the parking area. It climbs the rocky bank and quickly reaches the USFS access road to Silver Lake. Turn right, and follow the road uphill on easy grades. You soon reach a signpost that indicates you are entering the Green Mountain National Forest Silver Lake Recreation Area, advising that motorized vehicles

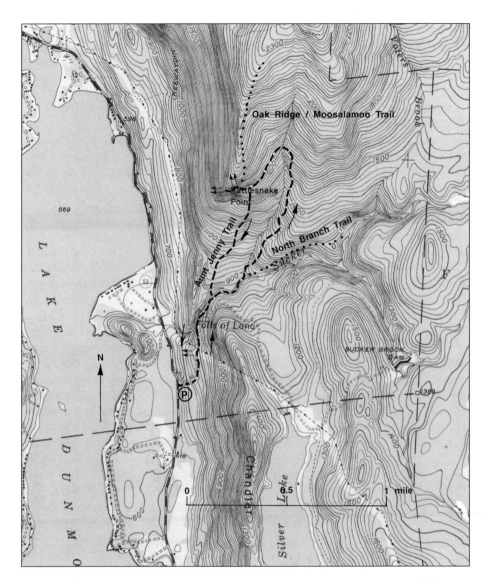

are prohibited in order to "preserve the quiet so seldom found in today's world." It also indicates a distance of 0.5 mile to the Falls of Lana and 1.5 miles to Silver Lake.

Ascend the road along switchbacks until you enter a clearing where a power line and penstock descend from Silver Lake to a power station on VT 53 below. (A penstock is a pipe that carries water, usually downhill, to a turbine to generate power.) Through the clearing are views down to Lake Dunmore. Beyond the power-line cut, the road begins a gradual ascent and soon reaches a wooden sign on your left as you start to hear Sucker Brook and the Falls of Lana. Take a minute to enjoy the view of the falls, which you can see from a short trail behind the sign. The Falls of Lana were discovered in 1850 and named by a party of soldiers for their commander, General Wool, who, during a tour of duty in Mexico, was known as General Lana, the Spanish word for wool.

Continue your hike along the road parallel to Sucker Brook until you reach the Silver Lake Trail junction and a large privy at 0.5 mile. Keep left, parallel to the brook, and then cross a wooden bridge over the brook less than 100 yards from the junction. Just beyond the bridge the trail swings up and to the right, passing over a campsite along the brook. You'll soon reach another trail junction, which leads straight ahead to the Rattlesnake Cliffs Trail.

Hike along Sucker Brook on the sometimes blue-blazed Rattlesnake Cliffs Trail. You soon reach a junction with the lower end of the Aunt Jenny Trail, which will be your return route. Past this junction, continue on the Rattlesnake Cliffs Trail on the old road above the brook to a clearing filled with fireweed at 0.8 mile. The signpost at the clearing indicates the junction with the North Branch Trail on your right.

Follow the Rattlesnake Cliffs Trail left at this junction. Note the marker in the ground indicating that the Youth Conservation Corps constructed this trail in 1977. After crossing a small brook, follow the trail as it rises steeply and relentlessly on an old lane. After perhaps a half mile of steady climbing, the trail leaves the lane, crosses a small brook, and swings along the face of a large bowl-like ravine. The trail soon reaches the upper end of the Aunt Jenny Trail at 1.75 miles. Note this intersection, because the Aunt Jenny Trail will be your return route.

Beyond the junction, the climb continues. Follow a series of diagonally placed wood steps, designed to help control erosion, steeply up the mountain. If you are hiking when there is no foliage, take time to enjoy the occasional views you get along this section of trail. At 2.0 miles, the Oak Ridge Trail, which leads to other trails and the summit of Mount Moosalamoo, enters on your right. Bear left at this junction, and continue along the trail, enjoying views of the lake below. You reach the junction of the West Cliff Overlook Trail at 2.1 miles. Take this trail for a view down to Lake Dunmore; then return to the junction. Continue on the Rattlesnake Cliffs Trail to the South Lookout, which descends to an open rock overlook of Silver Lake and Lake Dunmore at 2.3 miles. In addition to the gorgeous view, Rattlesnake Cliffs also offer a treasure of blueberries in season, so keep an eye out for them, as well. (*Note:* The cliffs may be closed to hikers between April and August if peregrine falcons are nesting).

After enjoying the view, reverse your route along the same trail to the junction of the Aunt Jenny Trail at 2.8 miles. In the early 1900s, hikers used to enjoy stopping at Aunt Jenny's Tea Room, a favorite resting spot and refreshment stand. Mrs. Jenny Dutton Rickert operated the tearoom, located just south of the Silver Lake Power Station.

Continue your hike by turning right and descending along the Aunt Jenny Trail, which is a bit steeper but passes through a beautiful oak forest. The trail is marked occasionally with blue markers, though you'll see a few pale yellow ones as well. At the trail junction with the Rattlesnake Cliffs Trail near the brook at 3.4 miles, turn right, and follow the trail over the bridge and back to the access road. From here, follow the road downhill past the Falls of Lana Overlook and back to the parking area at 3.9 miles.

24

Snake Mountain

Total distance: 3.5 miles

Hiking time: 2½ hours

Vertical rise: 980 feet

Rating: Moderate

Map: USGS 7.5' x 15' Port Henry

Hiking Snake Mountain is an adventure. Not only will you find a beautiful summit view, you will also enjoy oak forests, rare plants, old foundations and roads, and an area rich in Vermont folklore and history. While enjoying the views from the summit, consider that 14,000 years ago you would have been standing on an island in Lake Vermont! Lake Vermont covered this region from the Adirondacks to the Green Mountains except for a serpentine ridge–from which Snake Mountain derives its name.

Please respect other trail users you may encounter along your journey. Because the trail and summit of Snake Mountain are part of the 999-acre Snake Mountain Wildlife Management Area, hikers, skiers, mountain bikers, and hunters all use these multipurpose trails.

How to Get There

Go to the junction of VT 17 and VT 22A (0.0 mile) in Addison. Drive south on VT 22A for 2.9 miles to a left turn onto Willmarth Road. Continue on Willmarth Road to the junction of Mountain Road at 3.5 miles, and turn left. Go another 500 feet, and park in the lot on the left side of the road. Walk back down Mountain Road to where the trail begins at the end of Willmarth Road.

The Trail

The blue-blazed trail up Snake Mountain begins beyond the orange gate. Follow easy grades through an old overgrown pasture, where you will easily see the succession of

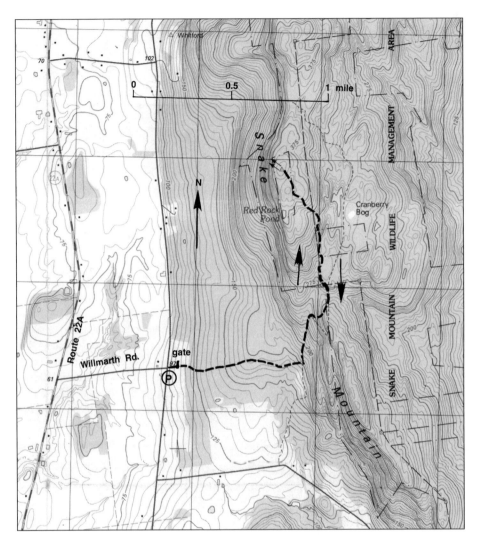

growth from former uses of this land. At 0.6 mile, the road reaches a junction. To your right is the former trail. Take note of this junction so you do not miss the turn on your return trip down the mountain. Turn left onto the blazed carriage road, being careful to avoid a faint trail that enters on your left. Occasional red blazes are property lines. In season this is an ideal area for beautiful spring flowers.

Continue your hike along the road, which begins to get steep and has deep water bars to control erosion. At 1.0 mile, the road swings right, then left onto a switchback along the steep bank. Avoid the old road on the right in the middle of the switchback. Please stay on the main road–the switchbacks are used to control erosion.

Above the switchbacks the grade moderates, and another old overgrown road enters on your right at 1.1 miles. Cross a small valley, and continue through an oak forest,

The trail up Snake Mountain

BOB LINDEMANN

where you will probably see an abundance of squirrels and chipmunks. Old roads continue to intersect the main route, so be sure to stay on the main road, which gets rockier and then levels off at 1.6 miles. As you near the summit, numerous old roads continue to intersect the main carriage trail. At 1.7 miles, the road swings to the west and enters a clearing at 1.75 miles.

The abundance of roads on Snake Mountain originated in the 1800s, when the mountain was the site first of a sawmill and then the Grand View House, which opened on the summit in 1874. The Grand View House was a popular destination for summer outings. In fact, for a time the name of the mountain was changed to Grand View Mountain because the founder of the summit house, Jonas Smith, thought the name Snake Mountain would discourage people from visiting his hotel. Mr. Smith also built two towers on the summit, first a wooden one and then a replacement made of steel; he charged his guests a fee to climb and see the view.

Life on the mountain changed a great deal in the early 1920s and 1930s. The Grand View House was permanently closed in 1925, the road to the summit was washed away in the flood of 1927, the hurricane of 1938 destroyed the tower, and the house eventually burned. The old foundation is well hidden but still visible if you explore the summit.

The concrete pad on the summit overlook is not, as many suspect, the foundation of the old hotel but rather the foundation of a house a young man attempted to build on the summit before he died overseas in a car crash. The state of Vermont eventually acquired the summit land in 1988.

From the concrete pad you can enjoy 180-degree views of Addison County and Lake Champlain, plus a view of Dead Creek below. Dead Creek, a spidery body of water surrounded by rich farmland, is part of the Dead Creek Wildlife Management Area and a favorite spot for canoers, duck hunters, and birders. The area maintains restricted and important waterfowl nesting areas.

If you choose to explore the summit area looking for old foundations and building remains, be sure not to get lost. After resting, enjoying the views, and possibly exploring, return to your car via the same route.

25

Pico Peak

Total distance: 5.8 miles

Hiking time: 4 hours

Vertical rise: 1,800 feet

Rating: Moderate

Map: USGS 7.5' Pico Peak

Pico Peak is a popular hike because of the fairly short, albeit sometimes steep trail that leads to an open summit with excellent views. The trail's proximity to a major road, however, means you may have plenty of company on your hike! The trail from Sherburne Pass to Pico Camp was the route of the Long Trail (LT) from 1913 until 1999, when it was moved west to avoid possible ski area expansion. It even predates the LT, showing up on a 1893 map. It was used to reach the fire watchman's tower atop Pico Peak until that was moved to Killington Peak around 1965. Wooden posts for long-gone glass insulators that once held the watchman's telephone line can still be seen on at least four trees 1.1 to 1.4 miles south of Sherburne Pass.

The Inn at Long Trail, where your hike begins, is an expansion of the annex of the original Long Trail Lodge, the former headquarters of the Green Mountain Club (GMC), which was built in the early 1920s with a gift from the Proctor family. Standing on the south side of Sherburne Pass, the lodge was an intriguing structure—with a rock ledge wall, a huge stone fireplace, and the LT passing through the building. At one point in the late 1930s, skiers could actually ski from the annex across the road directly to the Pico Peak ski tow. Although the GMC survived the Great Depression in fairly good financial shape, restoring the trails and shelters after World War II was not so easy. In 1955, the club needed additional funds and decided to sell the lodge. Unfortunately, the lodge was destroyed by fire in 1968.

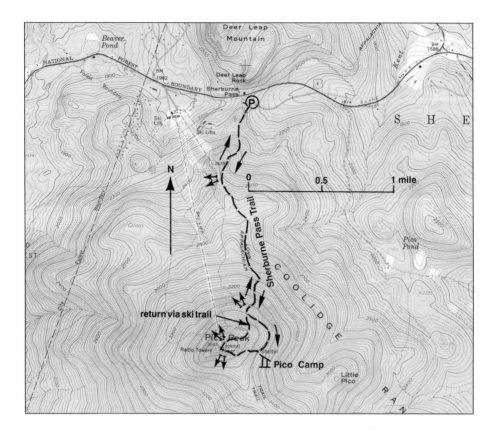

In 1992, almost 40 years after the lodge was sold, the GMC established permanent headquarters on VT 100 in Waterbury Center. Once again, Vermonters, visitors, club members, and volunteers have a comfortable and central place to gather for hiking and outdoor recreation information and events. The GMC also opened the Marvin B. Gameroff Hiker Center, which annually responds to thousands of requests from around the country.

How to Get There

Take US 4 to the top of Sherburne Pass (9.1 miles east of US 7 in Rutland). On the south side of the road, opposite the Inn at Long Trail, you will find ample parking.

The Trail

Take the trail directly behind the parking lot. Walk south on an old road to Pico Pond 0.1 mile until you reach a registration box where the blue-blazed Sherburne Pass Trail bears right and begins to ascend. You will soon reach a Killington Section sign from around 1966 that states that this section of the LT is "dumpless." This sign was erected because hikers used to bury their trash at a dump near each shelter. The sign now serves as a reminder of the GMC policy: PACK IT IN, PACK IT OUT!, which the Killington Section pioneered. Another Killington Section sign said, IF YOU CAN'T TAKE IT WITH YOU, DON'T GO!

On a moderate grade, you ascend onto

a ridge, and at 0.7 mile reach a spur leading right 0.1 mile to a view of Pico Ski Area from a 2,638-foot peak with a chairlift. The noise you may hear is the alpine slide, which operates during the summer. Bear left, and continue on easy grades. Enjoy occasional, although limited, views of Pico ahead from an almost level section of trail. In spring, before the trees leaf out, this is a lovely area full of wildflowers. At 1.3 miles, the trail passes a 7-foot-deep sinkhole and then a 15-foot-deep sinkhole. A permanent stream disappears into the latter. Both are part of a small cave not safe for amateur exploration.

The trail climbs gently in mixed hardwoods and evergreens and crosses several brooklets. The trail then takes a steeper grade and traverses the sidehill on three switchbacks until it reaches the Summit Glades ski trail at 2.1 miles. Turn left, and follow the ski trail uphill for about 50 yards, then turn left again and re-enter the woods. From this point, known as Pico Junction, there are outstanding views north to Deer Leap, the Chittenden Reservoir, and the Green Mountains as far north as Mansfield on a clear day. Make a special note of the junction location, because you may choose to return to this junction via the ski trail.

After re-entering the woods, the trail is much rockier although fairly level. Watch your footing in this section. At 2.5 miles, pass a spring and reach Pico Camp. The Long Trail Patrol built this frame cabin, with bunk space for 12, for the Killington Section in 1959. The camp is a snug place to take a break before continuing to the summit of Pico. There is a view to the east and southeast.

Continue your hike behind Pico Camp following the blue-blazed Pico Link. This trail is very steep, but quite short—only 0.4 mile to the summit. After crossing a wide swath cleared for an underground pipeline (2.6 miles), you climb more moderately through stunted evergreens to a service road. Bear left for about 25feet, re-enter the woods, and emerge in 100 feet on the 49er ski trail. Continue on the blue-blazed trail to the left of the top of a ski lift, cross the porch of a warming hut, and reach the 3,957-foot summit of Pico at 2.9 miles.

The summit offers two extensive viewing points. From the ski trails to the north you can see US 4, Deer Leap Mountain, and Kent Pond to the right; to the left of Deer Leap are the Chittenden Reservoir and part of the Green Mountain range. Watch Deer Leap carefully—you may spot some rock climbers. Near the radio towers (please heed the KEEP OUT signs; the towers operate under very high voltage) is a southern view of Killington Peak, Little Killington, Mendon Peak, and Parker's Gore.

After enjoying the views, you have two return options to Pico Junction. You could return via the route you followed up, or, to create a small loop, descend along the 49er ski trail and then, 0.2 mile north of the peak, bear right onto the Summit Glades ski trail. Descend steeply via this ski trail to Pico Junction at 3.3 miles. From Pico Junction, return via the Sherburne Pass Trail to the parking lot at 5.8 miles.

26

Mount Abraham

Total distance: 5.8 miles

Hiking time: 4 hours

Vertical rise: 2,500 feet

Rating: Strenuous

Map: USGS 7.5' Lincoln

The spectacular views from the 4,006-foot summit of Mount Abraham make this hike one of the most popular in Vermont. On a clear day, you can see the Adirondack Mountains in New York, the White Mountains in New Hampshire, and the Green Mountain range from Killington Peak to Belvidere Mountain.

How to Get There

Start in the town of Lincoln. At a rock memorial marker in the center of town (0.0 mile), take a left (north) onto Quaker Street. Pass the town clerk's office on your right. At 0.7 mile, turn right (east) onto U.S. Forest Service (USFS) Road 350, and proceed up a long hill. At 2.0 miles, you reach a fork where you bear right, still on USFS Road 350. The road becomes much narrower. Stay left at another fork. Continue to the parking area on your left, which has room for six cars, at 2.7 miles.

The Trail

Begin your hike across from the parking area at the trailhead sign, which indicates a distance of 2 miles to the Long Trail (LT) and Battell Shelter. Enter the woods on the blue-blazed Battell Trail. Swing left, and ascend a moss-covered hill.

Cross a wet area on flat rocks, and ascend some steep switchbacks. Portions of the upper sugar lines of a nearby maple syrup-making operation can be seen off the trail. Over the years, Vermont sugar makers have produced more maple syrup per year than any other maple-syrup-producing

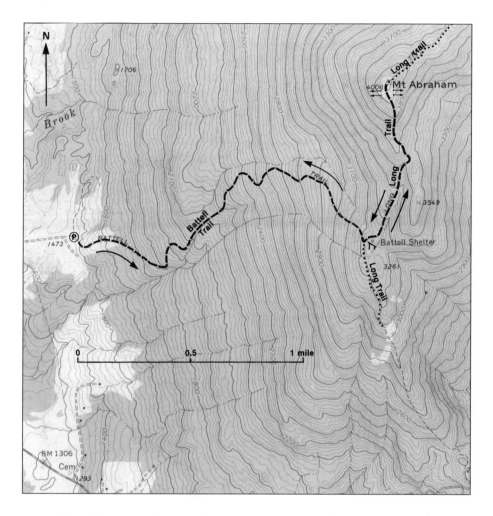

state: depending on spring weather, as many as 500,000 gallons each year. Approximately 40 gallons of maple sap, collected in the sugar lines you pass, produce just 1 gallon of pure maple syrup. Vermont maple syrup is required to have a heavier density than U.S. standards and to be free of preservatives. Look for "Vermont Maple Syrup" on the labels if you decide to take some home with you.

Leveling off in a beech woods at 1.0 mile, the trail diagonally crosses an old woods road and continues a moderate as-

cent to cross two small streams. Here the ascent steepens until, crossing a woods road once more, it enters another road at 1.2 miles and slabs across the slope at moderate to steep grades. The wide road continues uphill on a steep grade over long switchbacks. At the first left turn, note that birches, striped maple, and mountain ash have entered what had been primarily a beech-sugar maple forest. Spruces dot the slope. As the trail levels out at a spring (unreliable) at 1.4 miles, firs are found beside the road, and the forest is now dominated

---

Mount Abraham

by softwoods. Various species of ferns grow lush in a carpet of wood sorrel and club mosses, blue-bead lily, and Canada mayflower. The road, less defined because of erosion, may be wet in places. Cross a small brook at 1.8 miles, and then leave the road for only a short distance. Ascend the rocky, eroded road to the LT junction at 2.0 miles.

Hike straight uphill on the LT to Battell Shelter. The trail in this section, quite wide and on easy grades, follows an old carriage road built in the late 1800s by Joseph Battell, proprietor of the Bread Loaf Inn. Battell Shelter, constructed in 1967 by volunteers from Farm and Wilderness Camp using materials airlifted to the site by helicopter, has floor space for six to eight hikers and is maintained by the Green Mountain Club and the USFS. A small spring is located 60 feet east of the shelter.

Continue uphill on the LT along the very rocky old carriage road, with occasional views of the summit ahead. At 2.3 miles, leave the roadway and hike up steep grades, often on exposed bedrock scars. Look south, and enjoy views back to the trail you just climbed. Next, scramble up an exposed rock face, and return briefly to smaller softwoods before you begin your final ascent to the summit.

The trees are now waist high as you ascend to the open rock summit at 2.9 miles. A small rock wall provides shelter from the winds as you enjoy one of the best panoramic views in Vermont. To the east are the White Mountains of New Hampshire; to the west are the Bristol Cliffs, Lake Champlain, and New York's Adirondack Mountains; and to the south and north are the Green Mountains—from Killington Peak to Belvidere Mountain.

The summit supports a community of small, rare, arctic-alpine plants. The patches of "grass" are really sedge, and even the soil among the summit rocks is a precious commodity—without it, plants can't grow here. While on the summit, avoid disturbing any of these endangered plants by hiking only on the trail and rocks. For more information on this unique ecosystem, see the introduction.

Hike back down on the same trails to your car.

27

Mount Roosevelt

Total distance: 6.8 miles

Hiking time: 4.5 hours

Vertical rise: 2,100 feet

Rating: Moderate

Maps: USGS 7.5' Bread Loaf; 7.5' Lincoln

Mount Roosevelt is a healthy hike up the verdant Clark Brook Trail. Although neither easy nor difficult, it offers a steady climb for the hiker keen to access one of the fine summits in the Breadloaf Wilderness. Roosevelt's peak is accessed via a short journey along the Long Trail (LT) at the summit of Clark Brook Trail. The flat rocky summit has a largely undeveloped wilderness view to the north.

VT 100 in Granville provides access to the eastern base of the wilderness, with a short ride into the national forest via U.S. Forest Service (USFS) Road 55. The trailhead is just south of the scenic Granville Gulf Reservation. There are two waterfalls in the protected gulf and an ancient hemlock stand. Roadside stops there can easily be fit into the itinerary for a day trip that includes the hike.

How to Get There

From VT 100, turn onto West Hill Road, USFS Road 55, marked with a wooden sign at the very north end of the settled area of Granville. From the north, it is the first right turn after emerging from the protected Granville Reservation. From the south, it is the last left turn before entering into the Granville Reservation.

Continue straight, and bear left onto a dirt road, which will be well marked as USFS Road 55. Continue for 1.7 miles, past three right turns, straight into a small dirt parking area, or continue driving left across a bridge for a short way up the road to a second parking area past several

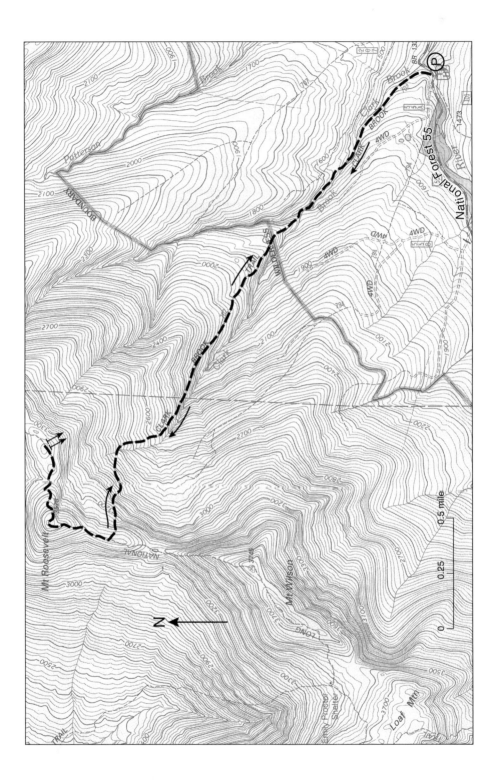

hunters' cabins. The trail is well marked on the right side, just past the cabins.

The Trail

After a short walk along flat terrain past several informal campsites along Clark Brook, you will enter into the Breadloaf Wilderness Area. Register here.

For the first mile, the trail meanders through the glades along the brook, and two fine bridges make your river crossings effortless. The bridges offer fine views up and down the deeply forested valley where glacial pools are sculpted out of rock.

After the second bridge, the trail ascends away from Clark Brook and begins the 2-mile climb to the LT. In the first mile of the climb, there are transitions of vegetation from the heavily shaded forest glade to the brighter fern and birch zones, where cloverlike oxalis and other ground flowers can carpet the ground at the right time of year.

The second mile of the ascent is characterized by small, rocky creek-bed crossings and a trail that narrows and steepens. Close to the LT, a well-built wooden ladder helps hikers to reach the top.

The LT is a major intersection at the end of Clark Brook Trail, with good signs directing hikers to Mount Roosevelt and other landmarks. Turn right. Follow the ridge featuring low scrubby vegetation and stunted spruce and fir with bunchberries, typical of the northern peaks of Vermont. It feels cooler here, and the footpath looks well worn. You are more likely to encounter backpackers and other overnight LT hikers here. It is always interesting to ask where they are heading and where they have hiked from.

After 0.4 mile, you reach the summit of Mount Roosevelt and just beyond, the rocky outcrop known as Killington View. It is the first full view of the surrounding Green Mountains as you head north from the Clark Brook intersection. The flat rocks provide a nice perch. The mountains are free of any development, and the view is of an undeveloped landscape of the northern mountains and forests of Vermont.

Return via the same route. As you descend the Clark Brook Trail, you can take more time to appreciate the ferns and silver birches and deep glades along the brook. The trail has given day hikers a solid 2 miles of healthy climbing, so on your return, relax and enjoy.

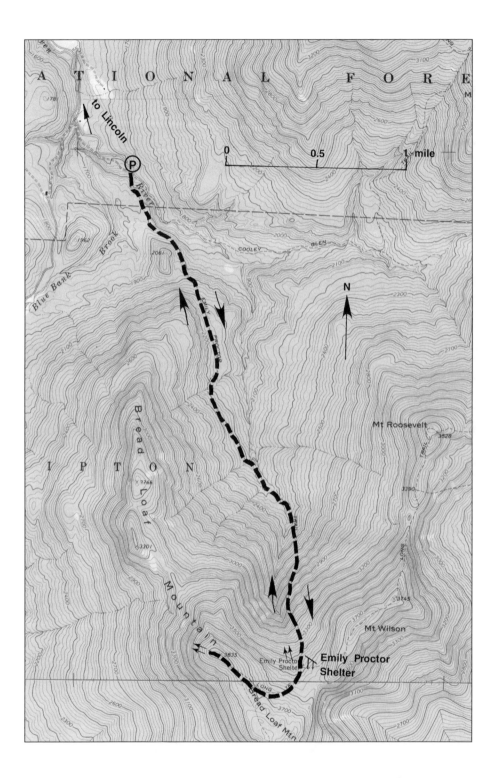

28

Bread Loaf Mountain

Total distance: 8.6 miles

Hiking time: 5½ hours

Vertical rise: 2,235 feet

Rating: Strenuous

Map: USGS 7.5' Lincoln; 7.5' Bread Loaf

Bread Loaf Mountain, so called because its long ridgeline profile resembles a loaf of bread, marks the halfway point along the 272-mile Long Trail (LT). An overlook near the wooded summit offers panoramic views to the west.

How to Get There

Take the Lincoln Gap Road, 1.0 mile east of Lincoln or 3.7 miles west of the Lincoln Gap summit, to the bridge over the New Haven River. Turn south onto the South Lincoln Road, U.S. Forest Service (USFS) Road 54 (0.0 mile), and drive 4.2 miles through South Lincoln and along the river to the junction of USFS Road 201. Turn north, and follow the road to a USFS primitive campsite and trailhead parking at 4.6 miles.

The Trail

At the trailhead, note the Cooley Glen Trail, which continues along the gravel road. Take the Emily Proctor Trail on your right, which begins with a steep climb along an old road. At the top of the hill at 0.2 mile, you begin to notice an open area on your right. The trail bears to the left. A logging road enters on your right, and you soon reach a hiker registration box. The trail then follows a wide woods road and enters the Breadloaf Wilderness at 0.5 mile. Limiting the use of signs and trail blazes preserves the wild aspects of the Breadloaf Wilderness. Motor vehicles and chainsaws are prohibited. Continue along the trail on easy grades with occasional views of the ridge on your left across the valley. This is a good section to

The Emily Proctor Shelter

stretch your legs for the climb ahead, which is rocky—so watch your footing.

At 1.0 mile you reach a brook that is a branch of the New Haven River. The Long Trail Patrol rebuilt this section of trail in 2001, eliminating two brook crossings. At 1.3 miles, the trail crosses the brook. The quiet pools here provide a welcome respite on a hot day. At 2.0 miles, the trail begins to ascend. Look for views of Bread Loaf Mountain on your right. As the ascent gets steeper, you cross several small brooks, and at 3.2 miles, the character of the woods changes from birches to spruce and fir. During the steep ascent, occasional level spots offer you a chance to rest and enjoy views of the valley below.

At 3.5 miles, you emerge from the woods at Emily Proctor Shelter and the LT, ready for a well-deserved rest. From the shelter there are excellent views of Mount Grant and Mount Abraham to the north. Named for an avid hiker and supporter of

the Green Mountain Club (GMC) during the early 1900s, the shelter is a log structure built in 1960 by the Long Trail Patrol; the Youth Conservation Corps replaced the roof and foundation in 1983. The shelter was repaired again by the Long Trail Patrol in 2002. The Long Trail Patrol was founded in 1929 when the GMC decided it needed a summer patrol to help with trail maintenance. The patrol, which still exists today, helps maintain and blaze the trail and reports on trail conditions.

Beyond the shelter, follow the white-blazed LT south across a brook and then along a gentle uphill. You will find this section of trail much easier than your climb up to the shelter. Wood sorrel covers the forest floor during summer months. Extensive trail work, including rock water bars and ditches to control erosion, has been done along the trail up the ridgeline of Bread Loaf Mountain. At 4.2 miles, the trail appears to double back on itself as you reach the now-unmarked halfway point of the 272-mile LT, a point very symbolic to end-to-end hikers. Take the blue-blazed trail that leads to your right. The wooded, unmarked 3,835-foot summit is a few yards along a spur trail. Continue to follow the blue blazes to the overlook at 4.3 miles.

This western overlook provides views of Lake Champlain and the Adirondacks beyond. The yellow buildings to the southwest are the Bread Loaf Campus of Middlebury College, home to the Bread Loaf Writer's Conference. The Breadloaf Wilderness consists of land originally donated by early 1900s conservationist Joseph Battell. To the south lies the Middlebury Snow Bowl Ski Area and in the distance Killington Peak.

After you have rested and enjoyed the views, hike back down the same trails to your car.

29

Mount Grant

Total distance: 8.4 miles

Hiking time: 5½ hours

Vertical rise: 1,960 feet

Rating: Strenuous

Map: USGS 7.5' Lincoln

The scenic Cooley Glen trail up Mount Grant follows old logging roads along the New Haven River. Although overgrown in places, the logging roads are dry and follow gradual grades, except for very steep sections near the top of the trail. Several swimming holes in the river provide the opportunity for a refreshing summer splash after (or maybe even before) your hike. Hikers will notice that the New Haven River is cutting deep into its banks in certain locations, requiring some trail relocations or adjustments. The bridge carrying U.S. Forest Service (USFS) Road 54 over the river, just below the trailhead was being replaced in 2002.

How to Get There

Take the Lincoln Gap Road, 1.0 mile east of Lincoln or 3.7 miles west of the Lincoln Gap summit, to the New Haven River bridge. Turn south onto USFS Road 54 (0.0 mile), and drive 4.2 miles through South Lincoln and along the river, crossing over it to reach the junction of USFS Road 201. Turn left here, and drive another 0.3 mile to the New Haven River primitive campsites and trailhead for the Emily Proctor and Cooley Glen trails.

Alternatively, from VT 125, 3 miles east of Ripton, follow gravel USFS Road 59, Steam Mill Road, north for 3.9 miles (passing the parking area for the Skylight Pond Trail at 3.8 miles). Turn right onto USFS Road 54, and at 4.2 miles, turn right again at a second junction. From here, keep to the right, and drive along the rough, dirt road,

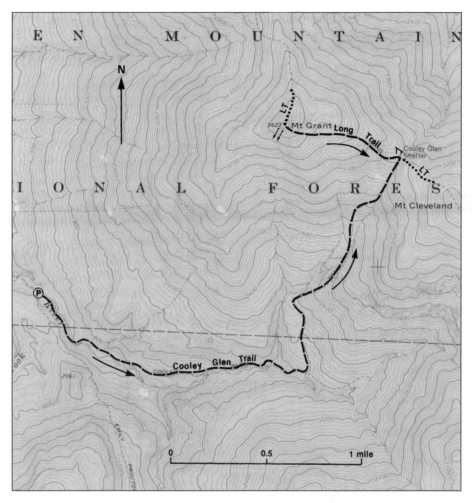

passing an occasional residence. At the bottom of a moderately steep decline (8.0 miles) and just before the bridge over the New Haven River, turn right onto USFS Road 201. The trailhead and primitive camping area are 0.3 mile ahead.

The Trail

At the trailhead sign, note the Emily Proctor Trail, which turns right. Instead, take the blue-blazed Cooley Glen Trail that begins to follow an old lane along the New Haven River, but soon climbs via a recent reloca-

tion above it to avoid serious river erosion below. Cross the river on a bridge at 0.3 mile (a trail register is here), and reach a clearing, once an old log landing. The trail leaves the far end of the clearing and follows the river on almost level grades over a wide, overgrown old logging road. At 1.0 mile, you cross several deep water bars and tributaries as you move away from, and then return to, the river. No blazes are visible along this portion of the trail, except for occasional blue-blazed rocks in the grassy road.

Mount Grant

At 1.5 miles, the road becomes quite wet and rocky. Enter the woods to avoid this wet area, and then return to cross a tributary. (There was once a bridge here, but this is revealed only to those who look closely at the opposite banks.) This point marks the entrance to the Breadloaf Wilderness, which was named for 3,835-foot Bread Loaf Mountain. Established in 1984, the 21,480-acre wilderness includes 17 miles of the Long Trail (LT), 11 major peaks (all more than 3,000 feet in elevation), and Vermont's Presidential Range (Mount Wilson, Mount Roosevelt, Mount Cleveland, and Mount Grant).

The trail now moves away from the river, ascends slightly, and swings left, still following an old road. Occasional blue blazes can be seen on the trees. At 1.9 miles, climb until you pass through a scenic, more mature forest. At 2.5 miles, the trail levels after a short ascent, and you can see Mount Grant through the trees on your left. The trail ascends steeply along a gully, passes through a rocky stinging nettle patch (wearers of shorts may experience a temporary itching), then crosses the small brook you could hear during your climb up the gully.

Now a steeper section of trail begins. You'll cross a small brook, pass a spur, and then reach the signed junction of the LT at 3.3 miles.

Turn left, and follow the LT north 50 feet to the Cooley Glen Shelter. The shelter, built by the USFS in 1965, is a frame lean-to with bunk space for six to eight hikers. Take time for a well-deserved rest.

Pass the shelter and continue north on the LT (the path just to the right of the LT is to the privy—recently rated five stars by a through-hiker from Alaska!). The hike to Mount Grant's summit is comparable to the grade you just climbed. Look for southern views before the trail swings right and you continue your ascent. By 4.0 miles, the mixed forest turns to predominantly spruce. The trees become more stunted as you hike along switchbacks to the southern overlook. The 3,623-foot wooded summit of Mount Grant is reached at 4.2 miles. From the southern overlook, a small patch of open rock, you can see the New Haven River basin, Mount Cleveland, Mount Roosevelt, Mount Wilson, and Bread Loaf Mountain.

Follow the same trails back to your car at the parking area.

30

Monroe Skyline

Total distance: 12.2 miles

Hiking time: 1½ days, 1 night

Vertical rise: 2,535 feet

Rating: Moderate

Maps: USGS 7.5' Mount Ellen; 7.5' Lincoln

The Long Trail (LT) between Lincoln Gap and Appalachian Gap (VT 17) is one of the most scenic ridge walks in Vermont. Named after Professor Will S. Monroe, who was instrumental in locating this section of trail, the LT from Lincoln Gap north to the Winooski River is known as the Monroe Skyline.

Your first day is a short 1.8 miles. This gives you time to arrange equipment and place cars at both ends of the hike. You should allow two and a half hours to reach the Battell Shelter before dark. If you get there in the early afternoon, walking up to the summit to watch the sun set is definitely worth it.

Start early the second day. Right out of camp, you begin with a short but steep climb to the summit of Mount Abraham. After that, you spend the day hiking high in the sky along the relatively flat ridgeline. From several vantage points along the way, you can enjoy spectacular views of Vermont, New York's Adirondack Mountains, and New Hampshire's White Mountains. After crossing Mount Abraham, Lincoln Peak, Nancy Hanks Peak, Cutts Peak, Mount Ellen, and, finally, General Stark Mountain, you finish your journey where VT 17 runs through Appalachian Gap.

How to Get There

Park a car at the top of Appalachian Gap. This is the height-of-land on VT 17 that is 6.3 miles west of the junction of VT 100 in Waitsfield and 9.6 miles east of the junction of VT 116 just east of Bristol. This is the car

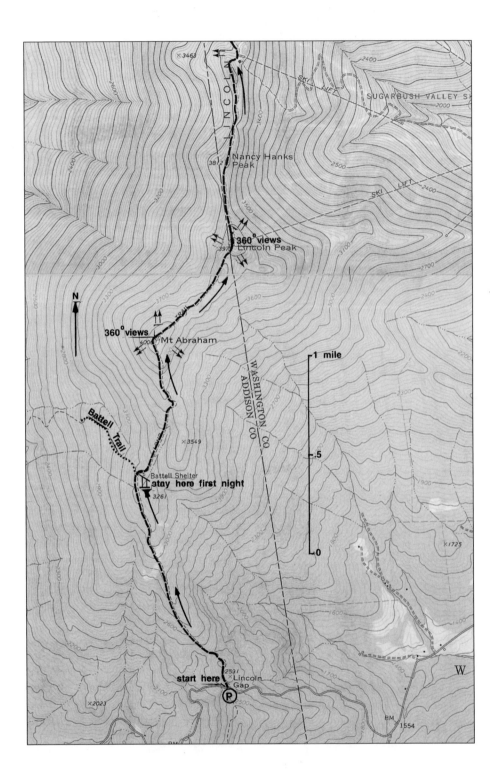

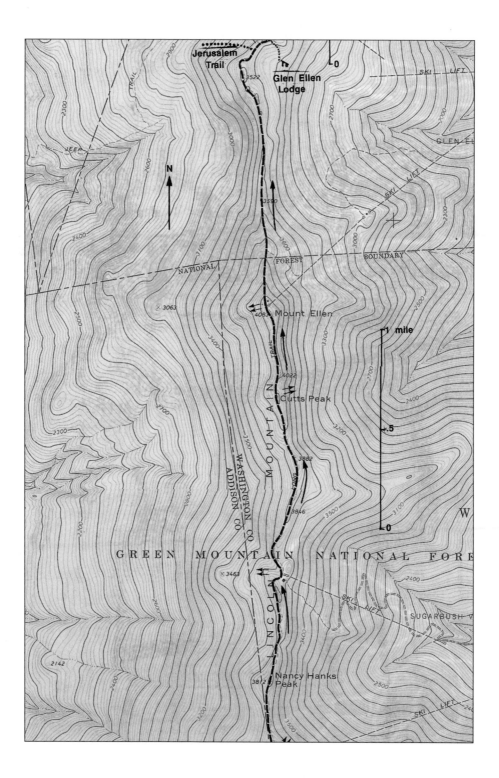

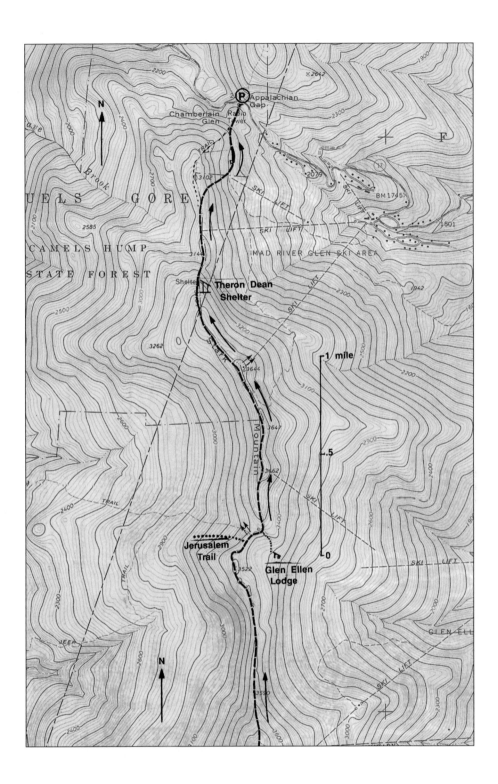

that will be waiting for you at the end of your hike.

To get to the beginning of the hike, take VT 17 east into Waitsfield where it intersects with VT 100. Follow VT 100 south to Lincoln Gap Road just outside of Warren. Turn west onto Lincoln Gap Road (0.0 mile). At 1.6 miles, the road turns to dirt. At 2.8 miles, the road turns back to pavement and ascends steeply to the top of the gap at 4.3 miles.

The Trail

Day One

Total distance: 1.8 miles
Hiking time: 2 hours
Vertical rise: 840 feet

Take the white-blazed LT north from Lincoln Gap. Make sure to sign in at the Green Mountain National Forest registration box. Except for a short side trip to Glen Ellen Lodge on the second day, this hike stays on the LT, which is reliably blazed white. Keeping this in mind will help keep you off side trails, which are blazed blue, and ski-trails, which are not blazed.

The trail from Lincoln Gap to Battell Shelter is quite steep in places as you ascend a series of plateaus. The trail starts in mixed hardwoods but quickly enters the boreal forest, characterized by a mix of red spruce and balsam fir that give the woods a pleasant fragrance. You should also keep your ears open for the numerous songbirds that make their home at high elevations. Prominent among these are the ever-present white-throated sparrow, tiny winter wrens, juncos, and blackpoll warblers.

At 1.7 miles you reach the Battell Trail junction. Joseph Battell, land conservator and former proprietor of the Bread Loaf Inn, cut a trail to Mount Ellen in 1901. This was possibly the first skyline trail in the Green Mountains.

Turn right at the Battell Trail junction, and ascend the LT to the Battell Shelter, where you will spend the night. The Battell Shelter was constructed in 1967 by Farm and Wilderness Camp (a local summer camp) volunteers and is maintained by the U.S. Forest Service and the Green Mountain Club (GMC). The shelter has space for six to eight hikers.

From Memorial Day to Columbus Day, the GMC stations a caretaker at the Battell Shelter. The caretaker is there to educate the public about the fragile alpine vegetation on the summit of Mount Abraham. He or she is also there to educate the public about low-impact camping techniques, protect water sources along the trail, maintain trails and backcountry campsites, and compost sewage to protect water quality. During the caretaker season, there is a $6-per-person fee to camp at the Battell Shelter. The GMC encourages all hikers, especially overnight visitors, to learn how they can minimize the impact that we have on the mountain environment. Please call the GMC Gameroff Hiker Center (802-244-7037) if you would like more information before beginning your trip.

Day Two

Total distance: 10.4 miles
Hiking time: 7 hours
Vertical rise: 1,695 feet

Your second day begins with the ascent up Mount Abraham. This is a challenging 0.8 mile of climbing. Make sure that you start at an easy pace so that you have enough energy to enjoy the long ridge beyond. After 0.6 mile of increasingly exposed climbing, the trail descends briefly to a signed clearing before making the final ascent above tree line.

The trees are waist high as you ascend to the open rock summit and one of the best

The view toward Bristol and the Adirondacks from the Monroe Skyline

panoramic views in Vermont. To the east are New Hampshire's White Mountains; to the west, the Bristol Cliffs, Lake Champlain, and New York's Adirondack Mountains; to the south, the ridge of the Green Mountains as far as Killington Peak. To the north, Mount Mansfield peeks out from the east flank of Mount Ellen. The summit supports a small, rare, arctic-alpine plant community. Please avoid disturbing any of these endangered plants or the surrounding soils. Walk only on the marked trail, and sit only on the bare rock.

Beyond the summit, enter the woods, and continue along the ridge until you reach the summit of Little Abe and then the 3,975-foot summit of Lincoln Peak—with a viewing platform just east of the LT— at 1.6 miles.

After you have enjoyed the summit of Lincoln Peak, follow the left edge of the ski clearing. Approximately 50 yards after you enter the clearing, the trail re-enters the woods through a small gap. Look for the

sign and white blazes marking the trail. For the entire day, it is important to remember that all ski trails between Lincoln Gap and Appalachian Gap go to the right (or east), whereas the LT is always the leftmost trail. The ridge between Lincoln Peak and General Stark Mountain is excellent moose habitat. You should look for their large prints in the muddy sections of the trail.

Continue your hike over the rocky trail on easy grades until you ascend Nancy Hanks Peak (named after a member of a prominent local family) at 2.2 miles. The trail then descends to the Castlerock chairlift. Bear left, and follow the ski trail 100 yards to Holt Hollow, where the trail enters the woods at 3.0 miles. A small spring is located 200 feet west of the trail along a short spur that starts where the LT leaves the ski slope.

Ascend the ridgeline over rolling terrain to the summit of Cutts Peak at 4.1 miles. Shortly after Cutts Peak, climb to the wooded 4,083-foot summit of Mount Ellen.

Just past the summit is a ski trail clearing with excellent views. The trail out of the ski area is small and frequently unsigned. The LT descends steeply to the left, just before a large board fence. Re-enter the woods to the left, and descend the steep western face of the mountain until you reach the northern boundary of the Green Mountain National Forest at 4.9 miles.

At 6.3 miles, you reach the Jerusalem Trail junction. Continue to the Barton Trail junction. This leads 0.3 mile east to Glen Ellen Lodge, which was built in 1933 by the GMC's Long Trail Patrol. The lodge has a reliable source of water, except during droughts, and is worth the side trip to fill water bottles, sit in the sunshine, or step inside on a rainy day to make some hot coffee or soup.

Return to the junction of the LT, and begin your last major ascent up General Stark Mountain. After reaching the summit, the LT continues along the ridge and follows a ski trail to the top of Mad River Glen's historic single chairlift at 7.9 miles. The trail passes Stark's Nest on the uphill side, briefly descends a ski trail, then bears left into the woods. You briefly re-enter the ski trail before returning to the woods. The trail between General Stark Mountain and VT 17 overlaps several small Mad River Glen ski trails. Remember that all ski trails descend to the east (right), whereas the LT bears left and maintains the ridge.

After a ladder that helps you over a particularly difficult spot, you will come to Theron Dean Shelter at 8.6 miles. Theron Dean was a close friend of Will Monroe and an active member of the GMC during the club's early years. The shelter is actually on a short spur to the left of the LT. The trail passes to the right of the shelter clearing. There is no water source at Theron Dean Shelter. After resting at the shelter, it is worth your while to explore Dean Cave, a short underground passage that leads back to the main trail 150 feet from the upper junction.

After Theron Dean Shelter, you come to one last chairlift. The LT bears left into the woods across a perennially muddy patch and ascends a small rock face. Follow the trail on long switchbacks through a scenic birch forest. Then climb over one final knob before descending to VT 17 at Appalachian Gap at 10.4 miles and the end of your hike.

31

Appalachian Trail: Sherburne Pass to Woodstock

Total distance: 22.3 miles

Hiking time: 2 full days

Vertical rise: 5,160 feet

Rating: Strenuous

Maps: USGS 7.5' Pico Peak; 7.5' Delectable Mountain; 7.5' Woodstock North

The Appalachian Trail (AT) between US 4 at Sherburne Pass and VT 12 in Woodstock offers a challenging 2-day backpacking trip. While the Long Trail (LT) follows the ridge of the Green Mountains, the AT in Vermont follows rolling terrain from the Green Mountains to the Connecticut River Valley. You will hike over geological thrust faults, up and down steep slopes, across mountain meadows, along country roads, through a moss-covered gulch, and past bubbling brooks. Along the way you may meet AT through-hikers, who often love to share stories of their long journey from Springer Mountain in Georgia on their way to Mount Katahdin in Maine.

You will also be hiking through Vermont's history, beginning at the site of the original Long Trail Lodge and ending near the site of the first ski lift in the United States. Before David Dodge invented his endless rope tow at the site in 1934, skiers had to climb up the hillside in order to ski down. Now they could be pulled up the hill by a rope tow powered by a Model T engine! The first person to use the tow, Bob Bourdon, was a friend of the previous edition's author, Bob Lindemann.

How to Get There

You begin your hike at the top of Sherburne Pass on US. 4, but you must first spot a car on VT 12 in the town of Woodstock. From Woodstock (0.0 mile), take VT 12 north past the Marsh-Billings-Rockefeller National Park (0.5 mile). At 1.2 miles, pass the turn to Suicide Six Ski Area, and continue on VT

12. At 3.8 miles (0.2 mile before the Woodstock/Pomfret town line), look for a barn on the right. On the left side of the road just before the barn is a guard rail. At a break in the guard rail, a small drive leads down to a tiny parking lot along Gulf Stream. Because the lot only holds three to four cars, take as little room as possible to park.

To reach the trailhead at Sherburne Pass, take US 4 to the top of Sherburne Pass (about 9 miles east of Rutland and 21 miles west of VT 12 in Woodstock) and the Inn at Long Trail. The inn offers parking for overnight guests only. There is ample parking in an unpaved lot on the south side of US 4. Be careful crossing! Traffic moves fast, and you can't see far in either direction.

The Trail

Day One

Total distance: 8.6 miles
Hiking time: 5½ hours
Vertical rise: 2,130 feet
Rating: Strenuous

The hike begins from the top of Sherburne Pass, on the north side of US. 4. Take the blue-blazed Sherburne Pass Trail at the east end of the Inn at Long Trail's parking area (0.0 mile). You quickly ascend among some boulders until you reach a rock ledge that you drop below. Watch your step through this area, especially with a full pack. This is the toughest footing of the whole trip. At the end of the ledge, the footing improves, and the trail descends through mixed hardwoods, then climbs on stone steps. You can still hear US 4 below. At 0.5 mile you reach a junction. To the left the white-blazed AT continues "south" (actually north at this point) to Maine Junction at Willard Gap, where the LT heads north to Canada. You take the white-blazed AT "north" (actually east), which bears to the right at this junc-

tion and continues 468 miles through Vermont and New Hampshire, ending at Katahdin in Maine.

Beyond the junction, the AT climbs gradually uphill in boulder-strewn mixed hardwoods and conifers. At 0.7 mile, it passes 15 feet south of a view of Pico, Killington, and the southeast. Descending, it reaches a 100-foot unmarked spur to the right at 0.8 mile to an overlook called Ben's Balcony, named after Green Mountain Club (GMC) President and longtime trail maintainer Ben Rolston. Begin a gradual descent away from the ridge. In this section, you occasionally see old blue blazes along the AT. Do not get confused. They remain from the time that only the LT (older than the AT) was blazed white from end to end. Its side trails are blazed in blue. GMC members referred to the AT as a "side trail" of the white-blazed LT, and thus they painted this section with blue blazes.

Descending steeply at times, enter a hardwood forest and reach campsite 11 in Gifford Woods State Park at 1.6 miles. Turn left at the camp road, and follow it past the road to the facilities and then a maintenance road, both on the right. If you need water, the park is a good place to restock your supply. Where the paved park road swings left to the park entrance, turn right onto a 200-foot trail leading to VT 100. Turn right onto VT 100, cross it carefully at 1.9 miles, and follow a 100-foot path to the upper parking lot of the Kent Pond Fish and Game Access Area. Kent Pond was created by the dam at its east end in the 1960s.

Cross the parking lot, bearing slightly right to its corner, and enter an overgrown meadow. At 2.0 miles, cross Kent Brook on a bridge built by GMC Ottauquechee Section volunteers. Notice the scenic cascade on the left of the trail with views down to the pond. For about half a mile, the trail

---

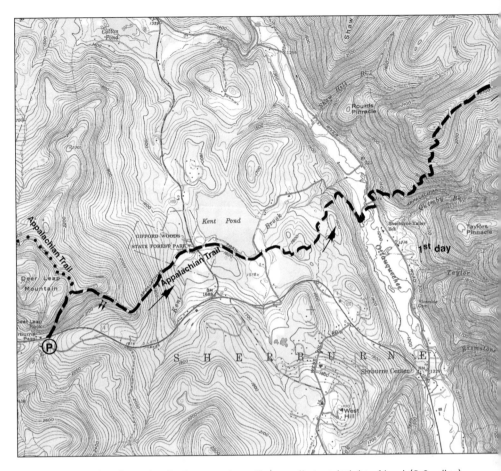

stays close to the shore. Look close, and you will see from the remains of two barbed-wire fences in big hemlocks that this used to be pastureland. Some of the shore is damp, but you have good footing on turnpiking (built-up footpath bordered by timber or rock) and puncheon (walkway made of boards or flattened logs). Pass through an old orchard, and cross a lawn, part of Mountain Meadows Resort, with a pretty vista north over the pond. Follow a path through apple trees, and then cross gravel Thundering Brook Road at 2.6 miles. You soon pass through mature pine woods, and then enter an area of glacial boulders, some bigger than a cabin. In rolling terrain,

climb gently to a height-of-land (3.0 miles), and pass through maple woods, ending with a very steep descent through switchbacks until you again reach Thundering Brook Road. Follow the road to the right, descending through what two stone walls on the left show was former farmland. Cross the headwaters of the Ottauquechee River, and reach an intersection with River Road at 4.3 miles.

The AT crosses River Road and goes into the woods. A sign at the road indicates you are almost at the halfway point: 4.2 miles from US 4, 5.0 miles to the shelter. Leave the road, and follow the AT uphill through switchbacks to a wooded 2,523-

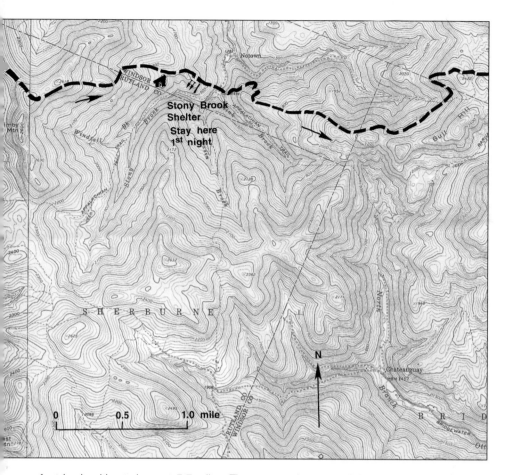

foot knob without views at 5.7 miles. Then descend through deep woods to a powerline cut at 6.2 miles with views of the Ottauquechee Valley and Killington Peak. At 6.5 miles, cross a wide logging road. About half a mile south is the former settlement of Quimby, remembered only by two cellar holes and a two-grave cemetery from the 1840s. Resume your ascent through more switchbacks until another wooded knob, and then follow a narrow ridge to the north peak of Quimby Mountain (2,640 feet, 7.3 miles), the highest point on this hike. Go over a slightly lower knob with nice white paper birch. Continue your descent along a narrow ridge, then through open hard-

woods to a gulch of moss-covered rocks and conifers. This gulch is a nice change of scenery from all the rolling terrain you have just traversed. At 8.6 miles, a 250-foot spur to your right leads to the new Stony Brook Shelter, built in 1997 by GMC volunteers led by Erik and Laurel Tobiason. Water is available at the AT's brook crossing just east of the shelter.

Day Two

Total distance: 13.7 miles
Hiking time: 8½ hours
Vertical rise: 3,030 feet
Rating: Strenuous

After breakfast, begin your second day by

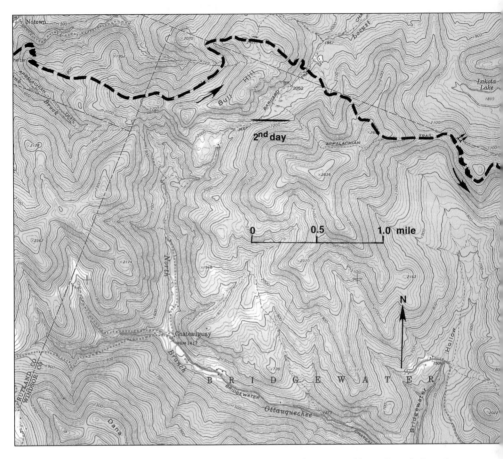

descending to a rocky overlook at 0.2 mile with a view into the Stony Brook drainage, followed by an 8-foot log ladder to help you down a steep ledge. (Dogs may have trouble here.) Descend steeply to a wide gravel logging road, then turn left and then right to cross a bridge over Stony Brook (0.8 mile) near an old log landing. From this point, the Stony Brook Road, passable in summer, leads north to VT 107. About 0.3 mile north on this road is Notown, site of a logging camp. Before loggers used the area, it got its name from the uncertainty whether the town of Stockbridge, Killington, or Bridgewater owned it, apparently through a surveying error. In those days, this was farm country, as house and barn foundations farther south on the Stony Brook Road attest. Once a year, everyone's personal property was taxed. This included livestock. To avoid the tax, the nearby farmers drove their animals into this area, where they could not be taxed because they were in no town.

Turn left again into the woods. After crossing Mink Brook, your route bears left and begins a steady climb on switchbacks back out of the Stony Brook drainage, reaching the crest of a narrow ridge at 1.4 miles. Climb more gently up a broader ridge and over several knolls. Pass a small pond, then slab along the north side of Bull Hill, crossing many old logging roads. At 2.6

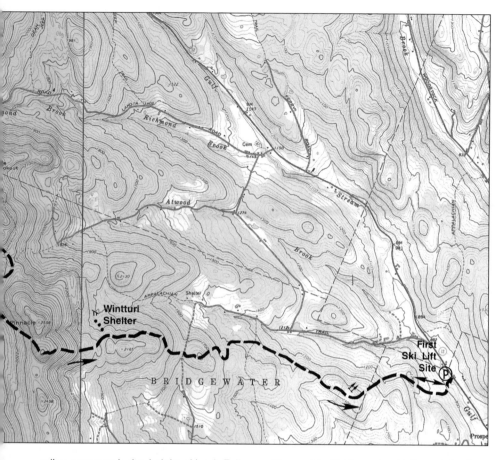

miles, you reach the height-of-land. Follow the trail down to a gully, over a few smaller hills, past several rock outcrops, and down a steep descent to the Chateauguay Road at 4.8 miles. In summer, this road may be passable north to Barnard. Beyond the road, cross Locust Creek and then some old stone walls that indicate former pastureland. The trail then begins a gradual climb, becomes much steeper through switchbacks, passes through a stand of white birch, and reaches a small clearing at 5.8 miles with a nice view of Lakota Lake and the White Mountains in the distance.

Descend from the clearing, steeply at first, and cross the old highway from Barnard to Bridgewater Hollow at the bottom of a gap. This road was abandoned before 1869 but is still a snowmobile trail. Then go uphill, over a small knob, through a beech forest, and along a ridge until you reach a trail junction at 7.5 miles. To the left a 300-foot spur, actually a road, goes to a private camp known as "The Lookout." It has a panoramic view over woods, fields, and mountains near and far.

The AT bears right at the junction and follows an old, eroded road that allows easy walking over gentle terrain. At 8.3 miles, it crosses an impassable old highway. East, this descends 0.4 mile to gravel Green Gate Road, where there is parking for about six cars. West, it descends to Bridgewater Hollow, an early but now mostly abandoned settlement. After following the old road 50 feet left, the AT re-enters the woods for a short distance and then, at 8.4 miles, joins and follows the abandoned King Cabin Road to the right for 0.2 mile. This road connected Barnard with Bridgewater Hollow. Leaving this old road, go over a ridge and reach Sawyer Hill at 9.3 miles. You then descend again, cross an abandoned road in a notch, go over a small knob, and at 9.9 miles reach the 0.2-mile spur trail to Wintturi Shelter, where you may wish to stop for water, which has been scarce since Locust Creek and probably will not be found again till the end of the hike. Erik and Laurel Tobiason and some of their friends constructed Wintturi Shelter, a frame lean-to with space for six hikers, in 1994. The shelter is named for Mauri Wintturi, an active GMC member and trail maintainer.

From the shelter spur, the trail descends a rocky sidehill, crosses an old road bordered by stone walls in a gap, climbs moderately, and parallels an old stone wall for about 425 feet. At the end of the stone wall, at 10.9 miles, a 150-foot spur leads to a vista of North Bridgewater, with a nice natural rock bench. Continue downhill through a stand of sugar maples and more woods with a thick understory of saplings. At 11.4 miles, cross another old road, bounded on the east by a stone wall and old barbed-wire fence. A more impressive sign of former farming is an approximately 45' x 40' foundation with a 7-foot-high stump of a chimney with north and south facing fireplaces, just northwest of the road crossing. As with all signs of former habitation, please leave it undisturbed. Descending slightly, cross a line of big old maples at 11.6 miles; probably an old boundary. Some of the maples along this part of the trail are 3 feet thick. Climb moderately through hemlocks to an extensive meadow, kept open by controlled burns, and reach a view of Mount Ascutney at 12.3 miles.

Descend moderately in semiopen hardwoods onto a rounded ridge. Junipers, another sign of former pastures, grow here. Passing in and out of the meadow, enjoy another southwest view at 12.5 miles, swing left, and re-enter the woods. At times you can hear the cars on VT 12. Descend moderately, first through big old maples with some huge pileated woodpecker holes, then through younger trees; then descend gently though a semiopen mossy area. Ascend gently along the south edge of conifers, passing some old barbed-wire fences. Slab the north side of the ridge, descend moderately to an old electric fence line in a draw, and then ascend moderately onto a conifer-covered hogback. Descend along a narrow ridge, where you can see a deep valley to your right. At the end of the ridge, at 13.2 miles, the trail opens into a large, old hill pasture with VT 12 in the valley below you. You can now see the first rope-tow ski area in the United States and the small building below that housed the base of the rope tow.

Continue down through the meadow following blazed posts, cross a gully and a former hayfield, and cross an old fence line with a wooden stile that is no longer used because the pasture has been abandoned. In July, raspberries are plentiful here, followed by blackberries in August. Cross into a cow pasture on another stile over an electric fence, hike through two more pastures, and finally reach Gulf Stream. Cross a wooden bridge built by GMC volunteers to the parking lot on VT 12 at 13.7 miles.

Camel's Hump from Mount Philo

M.L. RECOR

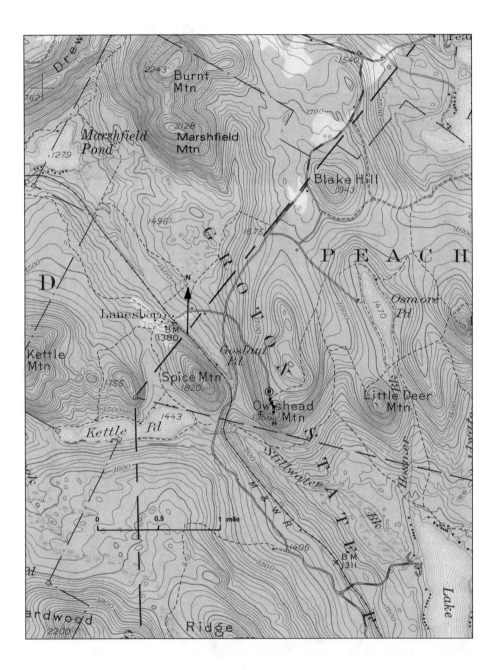

32

Owl's Head

Total distance: 0.5 mile

Hiking time: 30 minutes

Vertical rise: 160 feet

Rating: Easy

Map: USGS 7.5' Marshfield

This relatively short hike takes you to the summit of Owl's Head in Groton State Forest. The Civilian Conservation Corps (CCC) constructed the summit's stone fire tower, the trail, and the picnic shelter at the trailhead in the 1930s.

During the off-season, the 0.9-mile road to the picnic shelter is gated. The hike from VT 232 up the closed road makes a good snowshoe trip during winter's snow season and a firm-footed hike during spring's mud season.

The third-largest contiguous landholding owned by the state of Vermont, Groton State Forest is a scenic wilderness and one of the most popular recreational areas in northern Vermont. It has been used since the early 1890s for hunting, swimming, boating, hiking, fishing, berry picking, skiing, and, more recently, snowmobiling. Because the land was too rocky to farm, area residents used the region's forests of spruce, hemlock, beech, birch, maple, and white pine for fuel and lumber and to make potash for fertilizer and soap.

Since acquiring the first tract of land in 1919, the state of Vermont now owns approximately 26,000 acres in Groton State Forest. The Vermont Department of Forests, Parks and Recreation manages the forest for summer and winter recreation, forestry, and as wildlife habitat.

Exposed mountain peaks in the forest display a granite bedrock similar to that of New Hampshire's White Mountains. This forested wilderness supports a variety of wildlife, such as black bear, moose, deer,

The fire tower on Owl's Head summit

BOB LINDEMANN

mink, beaver, otter, fisher, grouse, loons, herons, and many other bird and mammal species.

How to Get There

Drive east on US 2 from Marshfield Village (0.0 mile) to the junction of VT 232 at 1.0 mile. Turn east onto VT 232, and drive past the New Discovery campground entrance at 5.4 miles. Continue beyond this entrance to a left turn marked by an OWL'S HEAD sign at 6.6 miles, opposite signs for Lanesboro Road and Ethan Allen Corners (during off-season the OWL'S HEAD sign is down, and the road is blocked by a gate). Turn left, and follow this steep gravel road to the parking lot and picnic pavilion at 7.5 miles. From the south via US 302, the Owl's Head road is 8.2 miles north on VT 232.

The Trail

From the parking lot, turn right, and walk to the large picnic shelter where a seasonal signboard describes the summer activities and programs as well as hiking opportunities in the park. Take a moment to enjoy the view of Kettle Pond from the shelter overlook.

Your walk begins behind the picnic shelter and heads toward the outhouse visible from the parking lot. Turn right onto the main trail, and begin a very gradual hike through mixed hardwoods up the first set of CCC-constructed steps. You soon reach another set of steps as the trail bears left and then right. Be sure to avoid any side trails, and take time to notice the extensive CCC rock work.

At 0.25 mile you reach the top of Owl's

Head and the octagonal stone fire tower. A rock outcrop beyond the tower provides fine views of Groton State Park. Visible to your right is Kettle Pond, and to your left is Osmore Pond, between Big Deer and Little Deer Mountains. To the southeast are approximately 850 contiguous acres of mature, primary succession forests of paper birch, red maple, and aspen, the result of intense fires around the turn of the 20th century. This area is logged during the summer to disturb the soil enough to create an ideal seedbed for the favored species of paper and yellow birch. Directly south is a 200-acre northern hardwood stand being regenerated to encourage aspen reproduction. Buds of mature aspen trees are a highly preferred winter food source for ruffed grouse.

Returning back past the tower, take a short spur to the right that leads north to another view of Osmore Pond. Hike back down to your car the same way you came up.

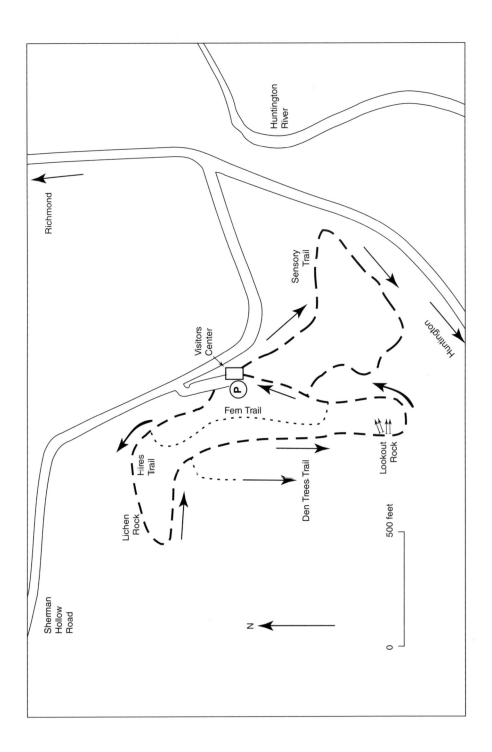

Huntington River

Richmond

Sensory
Trail

Huntington

Visitors
Center

P

Fern Trail

Hires
Trail

Lichen
Rock

Den Trees Trail

Lookout
Rock

Sherman
Hollow
Road

N

0   500 feet

33

Hires and Sensory Trails/ Green Mountain Audubon Nature Center

Total distance: 1.25-mile loop (total for the two hikes described)

Hiking time: 3/4 hour

Vertical rise: 200 feet

Rating: Easy

Maps: USGS 7.5' Hinesburg; 7.5' Huntington

Both of these easy trails are located in the Green Mountain Audubon Center, a 230-acre nature center owned and operated by the Green Mountain Audubon Society, a local chapter of the National Audubon Society. The grounds are open every day from dawn to dusk. The visitors center is usually open weekdays and weekend afternoons, depending on staff availability, and offers a Summer Ecology Day Camp, seasonal programs, workshops, classes, and more. We recommend that you pick up its brochure and map of the trails at the visitors center. Donations to maintain the center are welcome, and you can also purchase a variety of books and other items.

The Hires Trail goes to a lookout with an unusual view of both Mount Mansfield and Camel's Hump. The Sensory Trail, with a rope leading through fields and woods, is designed as both a hiking trail for the blind and visually impaired and as a way for others to enjoy and experience the area through their other senses. In addition to these two trails, there are several other trails open for walking, which are shown on the map available at the nature center. Please remember to stay on the trails, and do not remove any natural objects from the area. Dogs are not allowed on the Hires and Sensory Trails; dogs on a leash are permitted on some of the trails across the road from the visitors center.

Just 0.5 mile past the nature center on Sherman Hollow Road is the Birds of Vermont Museum, which displays hundreds of woodcarvings of birds by founder Bob

Spear, as well as paintings and photographs of birds and a bird-feeding station frequented by wild birds. The museum is open daily from May 1 to October 31 from 10 A.M. to 4 P.M. Admission is $4 for adults.

How to Get There

To reach the Green Mountain Audubon Center, take exit 11 off I-89 (0.0 mile), and take US 2 east to Richmond. At the traffic light, turn right (south) onto Bridge Street toward Huntington. At 0.3 mile, cross the Winooski River. The road bears right and winds uphill before leveling again. Stay on the main road as it bears left at two junctions. At 5.1 miles, you reach a sign and turn right onto Sherman Hollow Road. The center is the first building on the left. Parking for 8 to 10 cars is available, and a trail signboard shows the location of the numerous hiking trails.

The Trails

Hires Trail: This trail was named for Christine L. Hires, who donated the land for the center. The trail starts to the right, behind the signboard in the parking lot. Hike up a short bank, and bear right. Notice that you are hiking parallel to Sherman Hollow Road as you walk up the hillside through mixed forest on moderate grades. You soon bear left at the junction with the Brook Trail and climb through birches and then small softwoods.

Continue uphill to a spur trail on your right that leads to Lichen Rock, a large moss-covered boulder. Return to the main trail and quickly reach a junction. Follow the unblazed main trail uphill along several rock outcrops through a hemlock forest. Pass the junction with the Bob Spear's Founder's Trail, and reach a rock shelf called Lookout Rock at 0.4 mile. Enjoy the nice views of Camel's Hump and an unusual view of Mount Mansfield to your left. From the overlook, gradually descend through mixed forest until you are below the overlook. Begin a moderate descent to a junction with the Sensory Trail on your right. Leave the woods, enter an overgrown field, cross a mowed lawn, and reach the visitors center at 0.7 mile.

Sensory Trail: This unique 0.5-mile-loop trail begins on the porch of the visitors center, crosses fields, and winds through the woods. What makes the trail unique is its design for the blind and visually impaired. A rope, strung between posts, provides a guide for the trail, and signs are in both Braille and large-print English. For those who are not blind or visually impaired, close your eyes and notice the difference without the security and benefit of sight. You begin to rely more strongly on your other senses and more fully appreciate the sounds and smells around you. Any description would be woefully inadequate—this trail must be experienced to be enjoyed!

34

Prospect Rock (Johnson)

Total distance: 1.6 miles

Hiking time: 1 hour

Vertical rise: 540 feet

Rating: Easy

Map: USGS 7.5' Johnson

This short hike offers superb views, including Whiteface Mountain and the Lamoille River as it meanders through the valley below and empties into Lake Champlain.

Before or after your hike, be sure to take the short walk through the woods to the east of the parking area to view the Lamoille River and Ithiel Falls, a set of Class II rapids where the river narrows between two cliffs.

How to Get There

From Johnson (0.0 mile), drive west on VT 15 to the Lamoille River bridge at 1.5 miles. Just before the bridge, turn right (north) onto Hogback Road, and continue to a five-car parking area at 2.2 miles on your left at the top of the hill before Ithiel Falls Camp.

The Trail

From the parking area, carefully follow the paved road northwest 0.1 mile to the Ithiel Falls Camp meeting grounds. Ithiel Falls Camp is a religious family camp with a series of cabins and buildings. Turn right, and follow the white-blazed Long Trail up the gravel road opposite the cabins and past a rock outcrop. Cabins from the camp are seen along this short gravel road. Please remember that you are on private property and should respect all lands and buildings.

The trail soon turns left off the gravel road and enters the woods. Cross a small brook, and ascend to another brook. Now following an old logging road, the trail zigzags up the hill. At 0.4 mile, cross a wet area on stepping-stones and return to the old road.

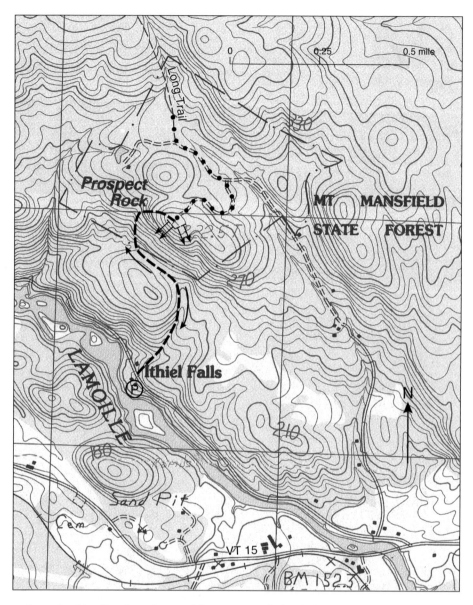

Large boulders line the trail as you hike on almost level ground through a forest of mixed hard- and softwoods. Climb along steep switchbacks, and then ascend more gently until you see the end of the Prospect Rock outcrop and enter an area filled with ferns. Pass under the cliffs, entering a rare, natural stand of red pine, a common plantation tree.

At 0.8 mile, the trail makes a sharp right, ascends the steep hillside, then levels off and summits Prospect Rock. Avoid the numerous spurs as you head onto the rocks. Our recent series of droughts have finally killed some of the trees found on the ledge.

Northern Vermont

MELISSA GREEN

Prospect Rock

The dry aspects of Prospect Rock contrast sharply with the river valley below. After enjoying the views of Sterling Mountain Range, including Daniel's Notch, with the Lamoille River Valley below, hike back down the trail to your car.

35

Mount Philo

Total distance: 2.0 miles

Hiking time: 1½ hours

Vertical rise: 650 feet

Rating: Moderate

Map: USGS 7.5' Mount Philo

Mount Philo State Park was Vermont's first state park, donated in 1924 by Mrs. Frances Humphreys of Brookline, Massachusetts. Mrs. Humphreys and her husband, James, were frequent summer guests at the Mount Philo Inn, located south of the state park entrance on Mount Philo Road, and they purchased 27 acres around Mount Philo in 1901, deeding it to Frank Lewis, owner of the inn. In the spring of 1901, workmen built the first carriage road to the summit, cleared paths, installed benches, and built a three-story observation tower on top. Mr. Lewis deeded the land back to Mrs. Humphreys in 1914 after her husband's death. The present entrance was built in 1929 and the road in 1930.

The Mohawk Indians had called the mountain *Tyontkathotha,* or "lookout place." Legend has it that the current name, Philo, was the name of a locally famous hunter and Indian fighter who camped along the hillsides and used the mountain as a lookout for hostile locals. Another theory has the mountain named during a burst of enthusiasm for classical names, hence *philo* from the Greek for friend or dear. Whatever the name, this small mountain has many big features: crumbly rock ledges, precarious drop-offs, and spectacular views.

In the 1930s, the Civilian Conservation Corps planted scots pine, red pine, Norway spruce, and other nonnative tree species on the side of the mountain, which was denuded from years of livestock grazing. An ice storm in January 1998 devastated the trees, and the park was closed that year

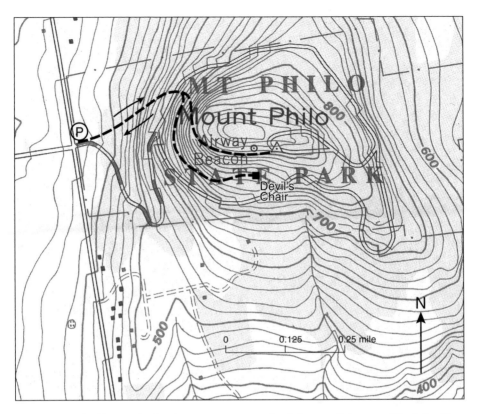

while mechanical harvesting equipment was used to clear blowdowns and remove dangerously overhanging limbs. The road also was rebuilt. Although most of the trees suffered ice damage, the native species, such as sugar maple, fared better than the non-native. It is a credit to the work crews that the storm damage and subsequent cleanup are practically unnoticeable.

In late April and early May, the hillsides and roadside are covered with white trillium, trout lily, bloodroot, bellwort, colts foot, rose-twisted stalk, white and purple violet, mullein, Dutchman's britches, and, of course, the ubiquitous dandelion.

How to Get There
State Park Road is located on US 7, 1.2 miles north of North Ferrisburg or 2.5 miles south of the stoplight near Charlotte. Turn east at the blinking yellow light onto State Park Road, and drive 0.5 mile to the park gate, immediately after crossing Mount Philo Road. You can park in the large parking area at the base of the mountain. From Memorial Day through October, the state park charges a day-use fee. Although the park is officially closed in winter, it has the distinction of seeing as much or more use in winter as a favorite destination for winter walkers and sledders. The paved summit road also makes an excellent mud-season walk while the trails are too soft for hiking.

The Trail
The blue-blazed trail, cut in 1996 by the Vermont Youth Conservation Corps, begins just beyond the gate and a signboard with a

---

Mount Philo

The view west over Lake Champlain

map of the park. It climbs steeply for about 100 yards, then gently ascends to an overhanging boulder known as House Rock. Climb moderately, then turn sharply right onto a switchback before crossing the "downhill" road at 0.4 mile. Continue uphill for 50 yards to a fork in the trail. Straight ahead a side trail leads 0.5 mile through a challenging rock maze under overhanging ledges to the Devil's Chair, a rock bench ideally suited for a romantic rendezvous or an afternoon with Emily Dickinson. Continuing past the Devil's Chair, this side trail descends past an old gravel pit to the "uphill" park road.

Back at the junction, the main trail bears left, climbing steeply around to the top of the ledge and a west-facing lookout. From here, the trail continues steeply, then more moderately to the first of many viewpoints—an open rock on the right—20 feet from the trail. Looking westward, you can see Thompson's Point jutting out into Lake Champlain, with Garden, Cedar, and tiny Picket Islands just to its north. The trail turns sharply left and continues uphill a short distance to the summit.

From the highest lookout point behind a metal railing, you can see Split Rock Mountain across the lake in New York. Looking southwest, you see Snake, Buck, and Shell House Mountains from right to left. Below you and to the south, the rooftops of the former Mount Philo Inn are visible.

You can return via the trail or by walking down either of the roads.

36

Black Creek and Maquam Creek Trails/Missisquoi National Wildlife Refuge

Total distance: 2.7 miles

Hiking time: 1½ hours

Vertical rise: Almost none

Rating: Easy

Map: USGS 7.5' East Alburg

These self-guided nature trails are in the 5,651-acre Missisquoi National Wildlife Refuge, which occupies much of the Missisquoi River delta and consists of marsh, open water, and wooded swamp. Missisquoi, an Abenaki word, means an area of "much waterfowl" and "much grass." The refuge was established in 1942 to provide feeding, nesting, and resting areas for migrating waterfowl. During the peak of the fall migration, there may be as many as 22,000 ducks present on the refuge at one time. The largest concentrations of waterfowl occur during April, September, and October. A variety of other birds are also present during spring, summer, and fall, including great horned owls, barred owls, ospreys, and an occasional bald eagle.

Remember to bring binoculars, and walk slowly and quietly so you don't disturb the birds and wildlife. Time needed to hike this loop will vary depending on how long you stop to observe your surroundings.

How to Get There

From Swanton (0.0 mile), drive 2.4 miles west on VT 78 to the National Wildlife Refuge headquarters on the left side of the road. Parking is located behind the office.

The Trail

Before you begin your hike, locate the large information board with a map of the refuge at the back of the parking area. A box at the board includes a trail map, "Black Creek and Maquam Creek Trails," as well as other information pamphlets. Note that the infor-

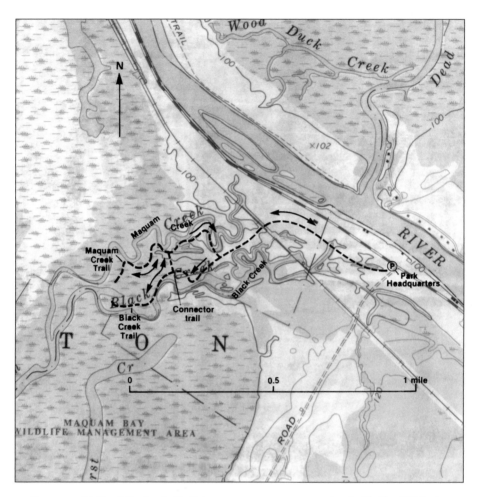

mation pamphlet's 1.5-mile trail distance does not include walking in and out on the mowed roadway.

The trail starts at the information board and crosses the large meadow and railroad tracks into a wooded area. You immediately begin to hear birds as you follow the trail along the wide, mowed roadway and across the railroad tracks. Through the brush on your left, look for a meandering creek and possibly some beaver activity. Also, watch for game trails, which crisscross this section of the trail. On your right, you soon see the remnants of an old, now overgrown

goose pen, constructed in the 1950s to establish a resident breeding flock of Canada geese.

At 0.3 mile, another mowed roadway, the Maquam Creek Trail, enters from your right. You will return by this trail. Continue straight ahead to the end of the mowed roadway and the beginning of the Black Creek Trail, which follows the bank of the Black Creek. Black and slow moving, the creek lives up to its name. If you wish, sit on the bench and take time to observe the reflections of the white birches, which make a nice contrast in the black water. Enjoy your time, but be prepared for a few (maybe many!) mosquitoes and blackflies during bug season. Look for the remnants of an old camp along the opposite bank just before the plank walkway begins.

At 0.6 mile, you reach a trail junction, where a sign indicates a distance of 0.2 mile to the end of the Black Creek Trail. Follow along the Black Creek bank to the end of the trail. Turn around, and return to the junction at 1.0 mile.

From the junction, take the connector trail to reach the Maquam Creek Trail at 1.1 miles. A sign indicates 0.5 mile to the end of this trail. Turn left, and hike parallel to Maquam Creek. Look for lots of ducks along the creek as well as nesting boxes. The trail may be wet and/or flooded at times.

At 1.6 miles, you reach the end of the trail at Lookout Point, with a view of the creek and marsh. Return to the junction at 2.1 miles, and continue east along the Maquam Creek Trail. The trail soon becomes more open and sunnier as you enter the mowed roadway. Just past a wet spot in the roadway at 2.4 miles, look for the junction with the road on which you entered. Turn left, and hike back to refuge headquarters at 2.7 miles.

37

Little River History Loop

Total distance: 3.5 miles

Hiking time: 2½ hours

Vertical rise: 880 feet

Rating: Easy to moderate

Map: USGS 7.5' Bolton Mountain

Established in 1962, Little River State Park occupies an 1,100-acre area within the 37,000-acre Mount Mansfield State Forest. The park's principal feature—Waterbury Dam—was built after two serious floods of the Little River in 1927 and 1934. The U.S. Army Corps of Engineers and the Civilian Conservation Corps completed the original structure in 1938. Officials anticipate to complete reconstruction of the current dam around 2003.

This hike offers a pleasant view into the past as it winds past abandoned settlements with stone walls, cemeteries, overgrown roads, foundations, orchards, and more.

A thriving community once lived and worked here. And, in the right place and the right time, it seems they still do. Early on a quiet summer's morning, with birdsong and cicadas chattering from the forest, the imagination can easily picture a sweat-soaked farmer cutting a field of sweet grass with a scythe. A teacher's voice drifts on the still air from the community's one-room schoolhouse. Smells of bread baking and apple pies cooling combine with the aromas from newly cut fields and blooming orchards.

This community lives on, if only in the imagination. Treat it with respect during your visit. Please take photographs of the area and any artifacts you find, but do not remove any items from the park.

How to Get There

From the junction of US 2 and VT 100 (0.0 mile) in Waterbury, drive west on US 2, par-

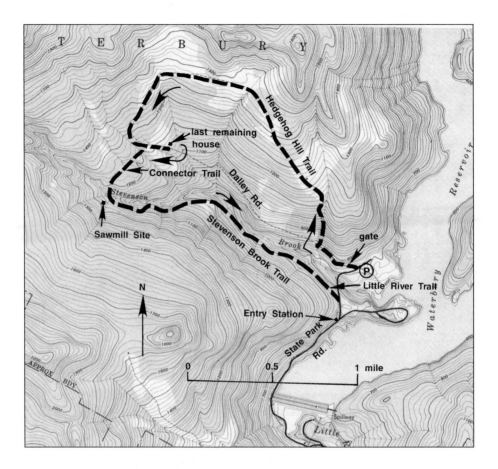

alleling I-89. At 1.4 miles, turn right (north) onto the road to the Little River State Park, and cross under the interstate. Continue to the Waterbury Dam at 4.2 miles. The road bears left, ascends the bank of the dam, and at 4.5 miles reaches the park entrance. The park charges a day-use fee and offers several maps and guides to the area. Pass right of the entry station, and bear left behind the ranger's residence. Continue on this road past the gated Stevenson Brook Trail on the left (the end point of your hike), and go across a bridge at 5.0 miles. Go past the NATURE TRAIL parking area at the bridge, and park in the small HISTORY HIKE lot on the right, across from a gated road.

The Trail

Leave the parking area, and cross the main road to the gated Dalley Road (a trailside box usually contains a history pamphlet). Climb gradually uphill along the roadway through birch, fir, maple, and hobblebush, as the sound of Stevenson Brook rushes to the left. Almost immediately, turn right off Dalley Road and follow the blue-blazed Hedgehog Hill Trail. At 0.3 mile, cross a culvert, and begin a short but steep climb. Wild violets often grow near the stream, as do hemlock and ferns. A large, flat rock at the top of the hill in a pine forest provides a sheltered spot to read the history pamphlet.

Little River History Loop

An abandoned furnace along the loop

A settlement of subsistence farmers lived and worked here in the 19th century, before they abandoned their pastures and the forest reclaimed the land. Today, only a sunken road bordered by rock walls marks the old pastures.

Arrive at the Gideon Ricker Farm (site 16) with an old road and foundation on the left (0.5 mile) and farm implements and relics scattered around the site. An optional route to the right uses a multiuse trail that winds through the woods, crosses several streams, and passes a deteriorating sugarhouse and an orchard before joining the Hedgehog Hill Trail and returning to the history loop trailhead.

Continue on the main trail as it narrows slightly, following the foundation between two stone walls. Wind through white birches until you reach Ricker Cemetery (site 15). Today native birch and hemlock crowd out the nonnative white cedar (also known as "arbor vitae" or "tree of life")

planted by the settlers to symbolically give life to the dead.

Beyond the cemetery the Ricker Lot Trail leads to the former Tom Herbert Farm (site 14), first settled in 1856. This site includes a stand of roses, two cellar holes, and an old well. The well, approximately 50 feet to the southeast of the cellar holes, is 27 feet deep. Approach it with caution.

Just before a clearing, cross the stone wall, and find yourself on the old road again, near the William Randall farm (site 13). At 1.0 mile, you reach the William Clossey Farm (site 12). Just beyond the farm, at the Kelty Corners junction, the Kelty Loop Trail enters, leading to Cotton Brook and the town of Moscow. Past the junction, on the right lies the Ricker Mountain School (site 11), one of five in the area. A lack of pupils forced the school's closing in the late 1800s. It reopened in 1908, but the school permanently closed in the early 1920s.

Continuing on the main road, go past the Patterson Trail junction at 1.3 miles. The James Carney Farm (site 10) sits to the right, and the Upper Cemetery (site 9) lies uphill in the woods. Beyond the cemetery, the trail begins a long downhill, past an obscure junction, until you reach a major, signed junction at 1.5 miles. Many of these multiuse trails include snowmobile routes and other postings.

Go past the sign noting the sawmill to the right; and turn left at the signpost following the main road. Before hiking on the Sawmill Loop junction on your right (1.7 miles), follow the main road downward 0.2 mile to visit the last remaining structure in the park. The Almeron Goodell Place represents the only surviving farmhouse in the Little River area. Almeron Goodell bought the land around 1864 and built the house of hewn timbers and hand-split shingles. One story of the time describes this disabled Civil War veteran as an escaped slave befriended by an area Goodell family.

After exploring the site, retrace your steps, and walk uphill to the Sawmill Loop Junction at 2.1 miles. In spring you might hear local birds—such as the brown creeper, black-throated blue warbler, and ovenbird— in the forest.

Turn left, and enter the a beech/birch forest, following old stone walls and across a gully. Again notice the old road and farm implements. Descend to cross a brook on rock stepping-stones, ascend a steep bank, and reach the junction of the Stevenson Brook Trail at 2.4 miles. A short spur to the right leads to the remains of the Waterbury Last Block Company Sawmill. Constructed in 1917, and in operation until 1922, two steam-powered 150-horsepower boilers ran this band sawmill. It employed 35 men, 44 horse teams, and one truck. Workers turned timber into ammunition cases and gun stocks, and hauled the finer wood to Waterbury for cobblers' lasts (shoe molds). Today, only a large boiler, truck chassis, and band saws remain.

Return to the junction, making sure to avoid the snowmobile trail beyond the sawmill. Return along the Stevenson Brook Trail, past a large maple, a grove with significant undergrowth, and trilliums, aster, and other wildflowers visible in season. Nettles also intrude on this overgrown roadway. The old road widens as you descend along Stevenson Brook and reach the abutments of old road bridges. Use the stepping-stones to cross the sometimes swift-running brook. The historical map describes these fords as "difficult crossings," although planks span some of the smaller streams. At one crossing, pass the remains of an old wooden roadway uplifted at a 45-degree angle. At one time, these spans provided a dry route for trucks and horses across the brook.

Some evidence of former settlements appears next to the brook, including a log structure. Beech and birch trees predominate in the woods. You soon enter a hemlock grove and reach an overgrown junction where the Little River Trail crosses Stevenson Brook. Continue descending along the right bank of the brook on the Little River Trail. Soon you bear upward to the right and leave the brook. Pass through the gated entry at 3.3 miles to reach the paved park road; then turn left and follow the road to your car (3.5 miles).

38

Stowe Pinnacle

Total distance: 2.8 miles

Hiking time: 2½ hours

Vertical rise: 1,520 feet

Rating: Moderate

Map: USGS 7.5' Stowe

This short, occasionally steep hike to a rocky knob provides extensive views of the entire Worcester Range, the Green Mountains, the Waterbury Reservoir, and the surrounding area. It offers visitors a comfortable hike, picture-book views, and an impressive vantage point overlooking local farms, forests, and the quaint resort village of Stowe.

How to Get There

Take VT 100 to the village of Stowe and turn east (0.0 mile) on School Street (directly opposite the Stowe Community Church). At 0.3 mile, bear right at the fork on the Stowe Hollow Road. At the next intersection (1.8 miles), go straight, and follow the Upper Hollow Road. The road then crosses a brook. Continue uphill, and bear right. Pass Pinnacle Road, and at 2.5 miles reach a state parking lot on the left (east) side of the road.

The Trail

This blue-blazed trail leaves from the back of the narrow parking lot, then crosses a field and overgrown pasture on puncheon (wooden beams that provide a raised, dry path over muddy spots). Volunteers from the Green Mountain Club and the Long Trail Patrol installed this puncheon—as well as water bars and rock steps you cross later in the hike—to minimize trail erosion and provide an improved footpath.

The Worcester Mountain Range and the Stowe Pinnacle appear directly in front of you; Mount Mansfield rises behind you. As

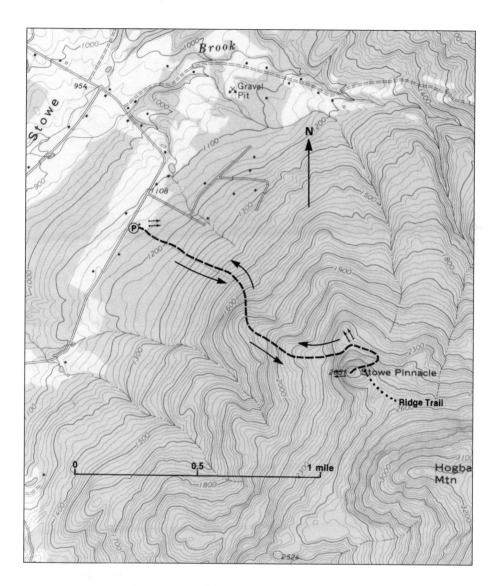

you enter a forest of young mixed hardwoods, please remember to sign in at the trail register.

You soon pass a large boulder, an erratic probably dropped as the glaciers retreated. The trail becomes quite rocky and begins to ascend. At 0.4 mile, cross a gully, turn right, cross another gully, and begin a steep climb through mature hardwoods. Look carefully

at the smooth beech bark for claw marks. In the fall and early winter, bears climb these trees and feed on beechnuts, leaving the impression of their claws in the bark of these "bear trees." You may also hear the staccato *tap-tap-tap* of woodpeckers as they search out insects in the trees. The insects invade the tree, woodpeckers weaken it with their pecking, and a strong wind

View from Stowe pinnacle

knocks it down, where the tree decays on the forest floor and nourishes new growth.

A series of switchbacks help moderate the ascent, before a sharp right turn leads onto a plateau. The trail swings left at 0.8 mile, and you ascend over an impressive series of rock steps installed by the Long Trail Patrol. As you reach the top of the notch, a short spur on the left leads to a view of Mount Mansfield and the Stowe area.

The slope below the viewpoint contains stands of sugar maple trees, from which local farmers harvest sap in late winter and early spring. Flexible tubing connects many of the trees, which the farmers connect only after the sap starts flowing on warm late winter days.

After enjoying the view, return to the junction, turn left, and continue following the main trail, which circles behind the viewpoint's ridge. The trail descends slightly, and then resumes its climb to the pinnacle. As you gain elevation, the trail becomes rockier; you'll encounter short fir trees indicating your approach to the summit. The Skyline Ridge Trail enters from your left, leading across the Worcester Ridge to Hunger Mountain.

The Pinnacle Trail bears right, and at 1.4 miles, you climb out onto the pinnacle with eastern views of the Worcester Mountain Range above you from Hunger Mountain to Mount Elmore. Western views of the Green Mountain range include, from south to north, Mounts Ethan and Ira Allen, Camel's Hump, Bolton Mountain, Mount Mansfield, Whiteface Mountain, and Jay Peak. The body of water in the foreground is the Waterbury Reservoir.

After enjoying the summit views, return via the Pinnacle Trail to your car.

39

Bluff Mountain

Total distance: 3.4 miles

Hiking time: 2½ hours

Vertical rise: 1,080 feet

Rating: Moderate

Maps: USGS 7.5' Island Pond

Bluff Mountain is one of those modest climbs that starts in town and fools you into thinking you'll be up and down in no time at all. But the trail takes a long approach to the summit and the nearby lookout area, giving time to tune in to the forest, which reveals both multiple timber harvests and the natural damage from the severe ice storm of 1998. The trail developers at the Vermont Leadership Center, working with the Northeast Kingdom Conservation Service Corps, designed the route to accentuate an understanding of this natural disaster, which damaged more than 600,000 acres of forest in Vermont and more in neighboring states.

The mountain is located north of Island Pond, also known as Brighton (its official name), in Essex County. With an unassuming elevation of 2,780 feet, it gets less hiking attention than more impressive mountains, yet it offers a good woods tramp and unusual tree formations. The approach to the peak—which has been hiked for decades and recently rerouted twice—goes across some privately held lands, but it borders the former Champion Lands, which are the major public access forests in the region.

Island Pond served as railroad center for logging in northeastern Vermont, linking the region to both Canada and Maine. The climb up Bluff gives a striking vista of the still-existing rail lines. Geologically, the mountain is part of the Gile Mountain Formation, technically not part of the Green Mountains at all. At the peak there's a

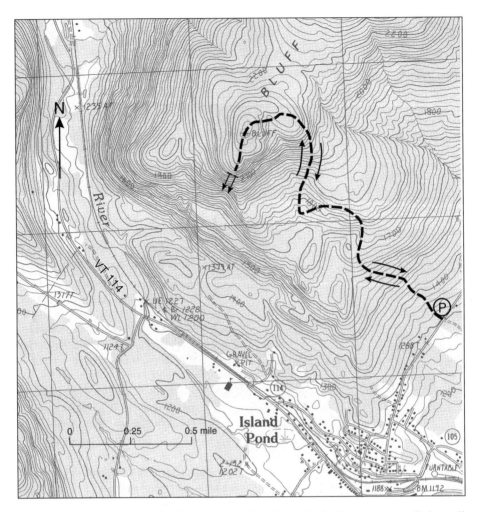

chance to explore the underlying stone, which is quartz-mica schist. A display at the trailhead orients hikers to this small mountain's assets.

How to Get There

At the railroad depot in Island Pond's center of town, take VT 105 east across the railroad tracks, and turn immediately left, then right onto Mountain Street. Continue on Mountain Street to where the pavement ends and an additional half mile to the well-marked parking area and trailhead on the left. At a pinch, four cars can fit here. If bringing a larger group, plan to meet at the railroad depot and carpool to the trailhead. There is a signboard with trail maps and a trail register. Signing in will document trail usage, which is helpful when the local trail crews seek funding for continued maintenance of the route.

The Trail

From the parking lot (0.0 mile), watch the blue blazes closely for the first segment of the trail, which rises through a plantation of red pine that is so orderly it can be disorienting. Cross two small streams (0.2 mile) as you enter a mixed forest stand, where elegant birches and older trees add to the sense of wonder that this gentle woods path provides. Cross an old logging road (0.4 mile), and note the transition for the downhill trip so you won't mistakenly follow it downhill on the return trip. A steady climb to the northwest travels through mixed hardwoods with few wildflowers. At the top of the ridge (0.6 mile), the trail bends sharply to the left and follows the contour line a short distance before turning west and crossing a small ravine. Looking south yields some minor views of Island Pond itself, as well as the Nulhegan Basin. Another bend to the left drops the trail sharply to meet the old route (0.9 mile) and illustrates the recent logging job that forced the trail to reroute in 2001.

A twist to the right takes the trail northward, past another early trail route, and resumes its climb up the mountain. Take a break here (1.0 mile), especially if you have kids along; the next stretch is increasingly steep. Note the stone steps and elaborately crafted switchbacks.

At the top of the rise (1.3 miles), the trail again changes direction, with a short downhill stretch followed by a sharp turn to the left. Begin a fresh series of stone steps and switchbacks for the strenuous ascent to the summit ridge. Views reward your climb.

The ridge at the top of Bluff Mountain includes a damp depression that you cross on bog bridges, where the views temporarily vanish; the actual summit is on a short spur to the right. The main trail bears left (1.5 miles) and continues on what was originally the Lookout Trail. Follow the yellow blazes through a moose hollow—yes, you will probably see hoofprints and mounds of moose scat—and then drop slightly downward to a fine vista (1.7 miles) of Island Pond, the railway, and the roads along it. Locate East Mountain by the odd buildings visible even at this distance on its summit. It once held a radar base that never quite reached significance, and it is now being considered as a wind-farm site.

Two variations on the return route can be taken. One is called the Lookout Trail and cuts along the cliff edges on the southwest side of the mountain. It's more difficult and can be found at mile 1.0 of the main trail, bearing left. The other is best saved for the trip down the mountain and involves bushwhacking (walking without a trail) from the foot of the upper set of stone steps, along the contour ridge, to meet the trail again, thus avoiding its dip to the former route. It's a pleasant way to enjoy a short try at orienteering, using map and compass, for about 0.2 mile.

The descent is not appreciably shorter than the climb upward, as the steep terrain requires careful footing coming down. Note the crossing of the woods road, which you spotted on your way up, and be sure to follow the trail, not the road. On your way back through the red pine plantation, some impressive stone mounds from agricultural use of this section become far more noticeable. Return to your car to complete the hike.

40

Spruce Mountain

Total distance: 4.5 miles

Hiking time: 3 hours

Vertical rise: 1,180 feet

Rating: Moderate

Map: USGS 7.5' Barre East; 7.5' Knox Mountain

This trail leads to an abandoned fire tower as well as several lookouts with excellent views of northern and central Vermont and western New Hampshire. Children especially enjoy exploring a very large split rock 1.6 miles up the trail.

Most of the trail up Spruce Mountain is located in the L. R. Jones State Forest, a 642-acre parcel of land located in Plainfeld. This forest—the first parcel purchased by the state of Vermont, on November 24, 1909—was formerly called the Plainfield State Forest. The name was changed to honor Professor L. R. Jones, a University of Vermont professor of botany, for his efforts to establish the state tree nursery and create the position of state forester. The summit of Spruce Mountain is located in Groton State Forest.

How to Get There

Take US 2 to Plainfield. Turn south at the flashing yellow light (0.0 mile), cross a bridge, and immediately bear left onto Main Street. At 0.4 mile, turn right onto East Hill Road, which quickly turns to gravel. At 2.0 miles, Spruce Mountain is visible ahead. Ignoring various roads on the left and right as you go downhill, at 4.3 miles turn left onto Spruce Mountain Road. At 4.7 miles, bear left at a wooden sign that indicates the trailhead is another 0.5 mile away. Continue uphill on the twisting and rough road, past a pull-off at the site of the old gate and parking area. Continue to the end of the road at an L. R. JONES STATE FOREST sign, where there is trailhead parking for as many as 15

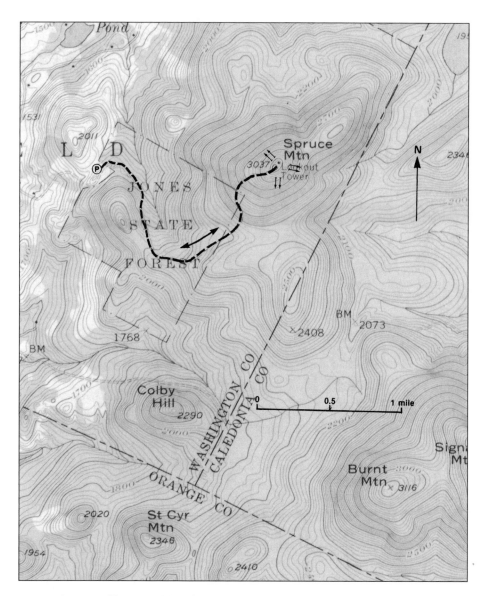

cars and a gate. Please park in this upper lot, which is located on state rather than private land.

The Trail

The Spruce Mountain Trail follows a path well-worn by fire wardens on their way to the tower. The first half of the route follows an old logging road, and the second half follows an obvious foot trail. The route is unsigned but is sporadically marked with blue blazes.

Begin your hike along the roadway past the gate. During this 1-mile road walk, notice the frequent views of Spruce Mountain, the fragrant spruce-scented air, and, in the fall, a few beautiful full-color maple trees along the way. Also, look for ruffed grouse in the woods—you may startle one into sudden flight. Although numerous old logging roads intersect the roadway, be sure to stay on the main road. Don't be concerned that you appear to be walking away from Spruce Mountain.

The wide road ends at an old log landing. Continue straight ahead, ignoring woods roads to the right and left, to pick up the old foot trail. You soon cross an unusual area of small, round rocks—or as one hiker describes it, "a baby boulder field." The relatively level, rocky trail continues past a large boulder engulfed by the roots of a birch tree. You soon cross a brook on puncheon, and at 1.5 miles, you turn right and climb a switchback to avoid an old, eroded part of the trail. The ascent is quite steep. The trail finally levels somewhat, and you reach a large rock outcrop split by the freezing and thawing of water. This is a good place to take a break and explore the rock.

The trail continues past the rock and ascends along a hillside by the bottom edge of a sloping, exposed rock slab. Follow the slab to 1.0 miles, where you swing right for a steeper ascent. The trail returns to a mix of hard- and softwoods and enters a small open area of ferns before returning to the woods. Climb a short distance farther to reach an overlook to the south.

Immediately past the overlook is the summit, with an old fire tower and the remains of a fire warden's cabin at 2.25 miles. The summit trail, cabin, and original tower were built in 1919. In 1931, the original tower was replaced, and in 1943–44, the current steel lookout tower was transferred to Spruce Mountain from Bellevue Hill in St. Albans Town. Although not used as a fire tower since around 1974, it was repaired and repainted in 1987 and placed on the National Historic Lookout Register in 1994.

A series of paths near the old cellar hole lead to various points on a rock outcrop that provide a nice view of Groton State Forest, including Pigeon and Noyes Ponds. From the tower, enjoy extensive views of central Vermont and the Green Mountain range to the west. To the east, Mount Moosilauke, the Franconia Range, and the Presidential Range in western New Hampshire are all visible.

After enjoying the views, hike back down the same trail to your car.

41

Elmore Mountain and Balanced Rock

Total distance: 4.5 miles

Hiking time: 3 hours

Vertical rise: 1,470 feet

Rating: Moderate

Map: USGS 7.5' Morrisville

Good views, a refurbished fire tower, old stone foundations, a glacial boulder, and a beautiful lake at the foot of the mountain make this hike a wonderful choice for a day of outdoor activities in Elmore State Park.

The park, which charges a day-use fee ($2.50 per person in 2002), was established in 1933 when the town of Elmore deeded approximately 30 acres of land, including the beach on Lake Elmore, to the state. During the early 1940s, the Civilian Conservation Corps constructed the bathhouse, a picnic area, and a summit fire tower and caretaker's cabin. This 706-acre park offers access to camping, a picnic area, hiking trails, swimming, boating, fishing, hunting, snowmobiling, cross-country skiing, and a winter weekend of dogsled racing. Lake Elmore is 204 acres in size and averages 8 feet deep, with a maximum depth of 15 feet. The lake is classified as a fair to good warmwater fishing area. The most-sought-after fish in Lake Elmore is northern pike; an abundant perch population has limited the numbers of other species. Little Elmore Pond is upstream and has better fishing as it is stocked annually with brown trout. Most of the park is forested, and the steep terrain limits the availability of commercial timber.

How to Get There

Elmore State Park is located on VT 12 in Elmore, just north of the center of town. In-season (Memorial Day to Columbus Day), parking is available in the park. From the park entrance, drive past the contact station and straight into the woods, ignoring roads

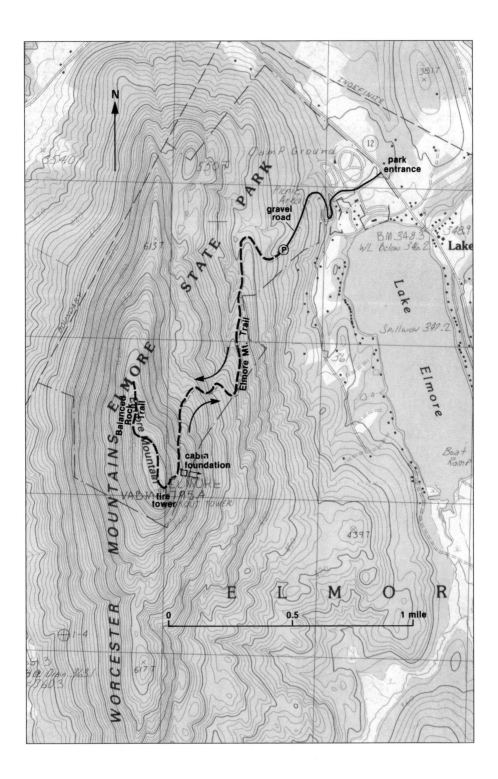

Elmore Tower from the clearing

on the left (to the beach) and right (to the campground). Follow the winding gravel road uphill to a turnaround and parking area at the end of the road by the gate. Alternatively, to add an additional 0.5 mile to the hike, simply park near the park entrance.

In the off-season, parking is available at the Elmore Town Garage, located on Beach Street, which leaves VT 12 a short distance south of the state park entrance. The town garage and volunteer fire station are lo-

cated a short distance down Beach Street, on the left. Be sure to park your vehicle in a location that will not block access to the buildings. An unblazed but obvious trail leaves the road opposite the town garage and climbs to the trailhead access road.

The Trail

The hike follows blue-blazed trails for its entire distance. The trail starts at the gate and continues up the gravel road.

Elmore Mountain and Balanced Rock

At the top of the first grade, an unblazed spur on the right leads to a beaver pond. Several other trails are evident, but the beaver-pond spur crosses a brook immediately and continues over a series of plank bridges. A pleasant 0.5-mile walk through the woods leads to a clearing with an old beaver pond.

Continue on the road past a rock cut and uphill to the end of the gravel road at 0.5 mile. At this point the trail makes a sharp right turn, climbs the road bank on steps, and enters the woods. Follow a gully uphill with a small brook on your right as the trail ascends with occasional views of the lake on your left. Be sure to stay on the blue-blazed trail and avoid the many side trails in this section.

At 0.9 mile, you switch back to the right and immediately make two steady ascents. At the top of the second ascent, pass through a rock cut, and continue over more level terrain. Next, cross a small brook on two logs, swing left, and ascend again. As you follow this gully upward, the trail terrain ahead looks very steep. Don't worry—the trail bears to the left and begins a series of sweeping uphill switchbacks.

As you ascend the last long climb, white birches appear ahead. At 1.4 miles, you enter a clearing, the former site of the fire warden's cabin, which burned in 1982. All that remains is the foundation and chimney, yet the flowers planted by the warden near the foundation continue to bloom each spring and summer. From the clearing you have a good view down to the lake and of the White Mountains to the east.

The trail continues behind the cabin site and begins a final climb to the summit. Be careful not to slip into the spring (the original supply of water for the ranger's cabin). The short summit climb is best described as a very steep scramble over rocks and roots!

Once atop the ridge, at 1.7 miles you reach an unsigned junction with the Balanced Rock Trail. Bear left onto the main trail, and continue a short distance to the 60-foot steel tower, which is in excellent condition. It ceased to be used as a fire tower in the fall of 1974 but was repainted and repaired in 1987 by the state of Vermont. The tower is used by birdwatchers every spring and fall during hawk migrations.

The spectacular views from the tower include the Worcester Range to the south as well as the entire Green Mountain range north from Camel's Hump, including Mount Mansfield. To the north are Laraway Mountain, Belvidere Mountain (with its asbestos mine "scar"), and Jay Peak. To the east is the White Mountain chain from Mount Moosilauke to Mount Washington.

After resting and enjoying the views, return to the Balanced Rock Trail junction, and follow this side trail along Elmore's ridge to a series of rock outcrops with beautiful views. The trail swings up and away from an eastern outcrop, climbs a shelf, and continues northwest over the ridge to a western outcrop. Continue along the ridge to the north behind the outcrop, descend slightly, and reach another outcrop with deep cracks created when weathered rock plates slid off the mountain. Be sure to enjoy the impressive views through these cracks. At 2.25 miles, you reach Balanced Rock, a boulder perched high on the ridge, left by a glacier that receded during the last Ice Age.

Hike back to the junction and down the trail to your car. After completing your hike, cool off and refresh yourself with a swim in beautiful Lake Elmore. The lake is also a favorite site for local windsurfers; you may be able to rent a windsurfing board and give it a try.

42

Mount Pisgah

Total distance: 4.0 miles

Hiking time: 3 hours

Vertical rise: 1,590 feet

Rating: Moderate

Map: USGS 7.5' Sutton Provisional

Mount Pisgah is located on Lake Willoughby and has sheer cliffs that drop to the lake. The cliffs have been designated a National Natural Landmark as well as a Natural Area by the state of Vermont. Approximately 993 acres of the area are permanently protected. Development, timber cutting, and road building are prohibited within the natural area. The geologic formation of Lake Willoughby and its adjacent cliffs are unique in Vermont. The lake lies in a trough cut in the granite, a fine example of glacial scouring.

The mountains are located in the 7,300-acre Willoughby State Forest, which was established in 1928. Much of the original purchase was once open farmland. In the 1930s, the Civilian Conservation Corps established plantations of Norway and white spruce as well as red and white pine. The forest includes hiking, cross-country skiing, and snowmobile trails, and six small cold-water ponds are annually stocked with brook and rainbow trout. Deer and grouse hunting are also popular within the forest.

Most of the trails in the Lake Willoughby area are maintained by the Westmore Association and its associated trails committee. Although the association formed in 1967, some of the Westmore trails were laid out long before that time. The Mount Pisgah trails are now maintained by the state of Vermont.

Mount Pisgah is located on the east side of Lake Willoughby. The trail parallels a steep rock face with great views down to the lake and the surrounding area. The orig-

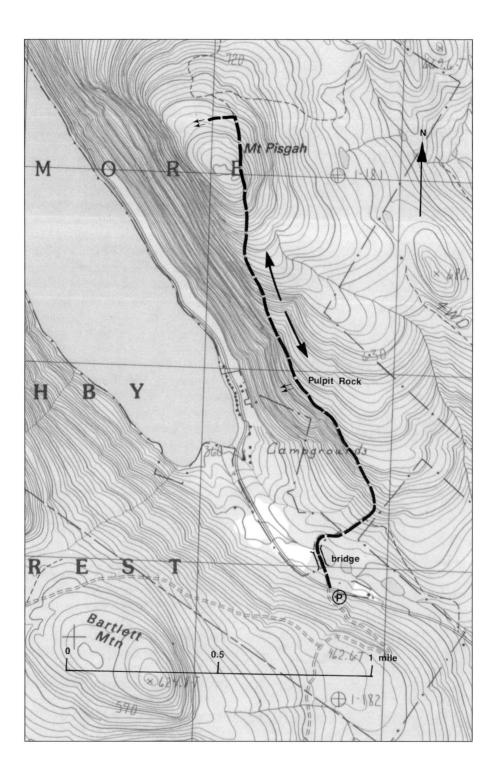

Beaver Pond at Mount Pisgah

inal "south" trail up Pisgah dates back to the late 1800s.

How to Get There

To reach the Mount Pisgah trailhead from the south, follow VT 5A north from its intersection with US 5 in West Burke (0.0 mile) 5.7 miles to the parking area on the left (west) side of the road before you reach the south shore of Lake Willoughby.

To reach the trailhead from the north or east, drive east on VT 16 from the center of Barton (0.0 mile) to its intersection with US 5 at 0.3 mile. Turn left onto VT 16, and continue to VT 5A at 7.3 miles. Turn right (south) onto VT 5A, and drive the entire length of the lake to the parking area on the right (west) side of the road at 13.0 miles. As you drive along the east side of Lake Willoughby, you can see Mount Hor across the lake on the right and Mount Pisgah above you on the left. As you might expect, this highway is sometimes closed by rockfalls.

The parking area with ample space for cars has picnic tables for lunch or a snack break, plus a signboard about the area trails. The trailhead sign on the opposite side of the road indicates a distance of 1.7 miles to the summit of Mount Pisgah.

The Trail

Cross the road carefully, and descend the road embankment on the blue-blazed trail until you come to a swamp. Avoid the faint blue blazes to your right. Instead, turn left, and cross a wooden bridge over the swamp. You can see occasional views of the Mount Hor cliffs. Climb the bank behind the pond, and follow an old road that bears right, away from the pond.

As you start to see a clearing ahead, the trail makes a sharp left and begins a long switchback climb. Look for a water pipe along the trail, and take time to notice the extensive maintenance work required in this area. You soon follow the ridge uphill on a wide, more gradual trail. To the left is the steep side of the mountain descending to Lake Willoughby. At 0.9 mile, look for the short spur to Pulpit Rock, where you have an excellent view down to the lake and of Mount Hor beyond. Be careful—you are standing on a rock overhang, approximately 650 feet above the lake.

Back on the main trail, continue a steady climb along the ridge, and then bear right. Moving away from the lake, you enter a maple forest, ascend the hillside, and hike through a birch forest. As the trail gets narrower, climb through boulders and skirt a ledge at 1.3 miles. You have now lost all views of the lake as you enter a softwood forest along the backside of the mountain.

The trail switches back until you find yourself at the bottom of a long rock slab. Climb the slab for a good view of the Burke Mountain area. Above the slab, you enter the woods and reach a spur leading to East Overlook. Continue down along the ridge until, at 1.9 miles, you reach a spur on your left leading to the Upper Overlook. Take this steep, muddy trail 0.1 mile down to a spectacular view of Lake Memphremagog, Lake Willoughby, Wheeler Mountain, Mount Hor, Jay Peak, the Green Mountain Range, and the surrounding area.

Return to the trail junction, and hike back down the main trail to your car.

43

Jay Peak

Total distance: 3.4 miles

Hiking time: 3 hours

Vertical rise: 1,680 feet

Rating: Moderate

Map: USGS 7.5' Jay Peak

Jay Peak, the northernmost high peak in the Green Mountain chain, was named in honor of John Jay, the first chief justice of the United States, who was instrumental in settling a controversy between the state of Vermont and the state of New York. The summits of Little Jay, Big Jay, and Jay Peak; 3 miles of the Long Trail (LT); and the Jay Peak Ski Area are all included in Jay State Forest, which is managed primarily for recreation, wildlife, and watershed protection. An enclosed aerial tramway at the Jay Peak Ski Area allows year-round visits to the summit, so expect a few other visitors. Lying to the west of Jay Peak, the 3,674-acre Black Falls tract was added to Jay State Forest in 2001, bringing the total holding to more than 5,000 acres.

How to Get There

The trailhead parking area for 15 cars is located at the height-of-land on the south side of VT 242, approximately 1.4 miles west of the Jay Peak Ski Area access road and 6.6 miles east of VT 118 in Montgomery Center.

The Trail

The entire hike from the VT 242 parking lot to the summit of Jay Peak follows the white-blazed LT. Begin by following the path north, up the bank opposite the parking lot. At the very beginning of the trail is Atlas Valley Shelter, a small lean-to not designed for overnight use. Made from plywood and plywood cores donated by the Atlas Valley Company, the shelter was prefabricated at

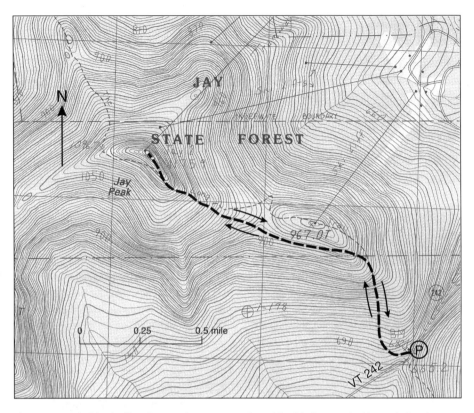

the company's Morrisville plant and assembled on the site by Green Mountain Club (GMC) volunteers in 1967.

Almost immediately, the LT reaches a signed trail junction where the Catamount Ski Trail and blue-blazed Jay Camp Loop hiking trail depart to the left on a shared path. The left branch leads a short distance to Jay Camp, a frame cabin constructed in 1958 and maintained by the GMC for the use of long-distance hikers. Continue straight through the junction on the LT, climbing gradually, then more steeply, through a hardwood forest, and continue past the signed north end of the Jay Camp Loop.

The trail turns to the west and climbs on moderate grades for some distance, eventually leaving the hardwood forest, first for the white birches and ultimately for the aromatic spruce-fir zone. There are limited views to the south and west in areas where storms have knocked over large trees, creating holes in the canopy. The LT turns left at 1.0 mile to avoid a ski trail, and then scrambles over some steep ledges and rougher terrain. The trail turns left again at 1.2 miles and begins a steeper climb over jumbled rocks until it emerges through a wooden fence onto a ski trail. There are good views here to the east and south, and on a sunny summer day the ski trail looks like a grassy alpine meadow. The LT continues directly across the ski trail (look for the white blazes on the rocks) and climbs steeply, at times scrambling up ledges, to reach the summit at 1.7 miles. As you climb into the scrub near tree line here, be care-

On the summit of Jay

Blue flag along the trail

ful to get your bearings on the final climb to the summit, so you can descend in the right direction!

On the summit is the upper tram station of the Jay Peak Ski Area. Please respect their buildings and property. On a clear day, there are views of Canada to the north, the Adirondack Mountains to the west, the White Mountains to the east, and most of northern Vermont. The large lake to the northeast is Lake Memphremagog, near Newport, Vermont. The summit of Jay Peak is exposed and can be a dangerous place in inclement weather. Limited shelter is available under the tram building.

You may simply descend the way you came; however, there are two opportunities to vary the route of your return. First, you can use the alpine ski trails to leave the summit to the *north* and loop back to the point where the LT crossed the ski trail on the ascent. To do this, from the tram station on the summit, follow the white-blazed LT *north* along an alpine ski trail, making a steep descent to a ski trail junction. Here the LT passes through a fence and enters the woods. Do *not* follow it! Rather, turn left at the junction, and follow the alpine ski trail to the southeast, passing a ways below the tram station. This is the ski trail you crossed on your ascent—so keep a sharp lookout on the right for the white blazes and a small LONG TRAIL sign, just after the ski trail begins its descent. Note that the ski trails are not blazed like the LT.

Second, you may vary your descent route near the bottom of the mountain by following the blue-blazed Jay Loop trail at its signed upper junction, where it departs steeply to the right from the LT. The Jay Loop trail passes Jay Camp and returns to the LT a short distance above the parking lot on VT 242.

44

Hubbard Park

Total distance: 5.75 miles

Hiking time: 3½ hours

Vertical rise: 374 feet

Rating: Moderate

Map: USGS 7.5' Montpelier

Hubbard Park is a quiet–even wild–place in the heart of Vermont's capitol city. The high point of the park is Capitol Hill, whose evergreen forest forms the backdrop for the golden dome of the state capitol building. The Hubbard family settled in Montpelier in 1799 and used the park land for various enterprises through the 19th century before donating it to the city in 1899. The city parks commission has created a few man-made additions to the park over the years, most notably the construction of an impressive observation tower on the summit of Capitol Hill. But the majority of the park has been left in its natural state. The park is mostly a second-growth forest with a mixture of hardwoods and softwoods. It has a variety of habitats, including steep ground with dry soil and plants unusual for the area, hardwood forest with moist soil and a high diversity of spring wildflowers, several marshy areas, and elevated, rocky cliffs.

In recent years, Montpelier City Parks has done excellent work connecting the trail systems of the parks and natural areas in the city limits. This has made possible a substantial new day-hike loop that connects historic neighborhoods, great mountain views, quiet forest glades, and wild natural areas, as well as grassy playing fields and picnic spots.

Hubbard Park is a great place to hike with your dog! Expect to meet many four-legged friends.

How to Get There

The trail begins at the Winter Street gate of Hubbard Park in Montpelier. To get there

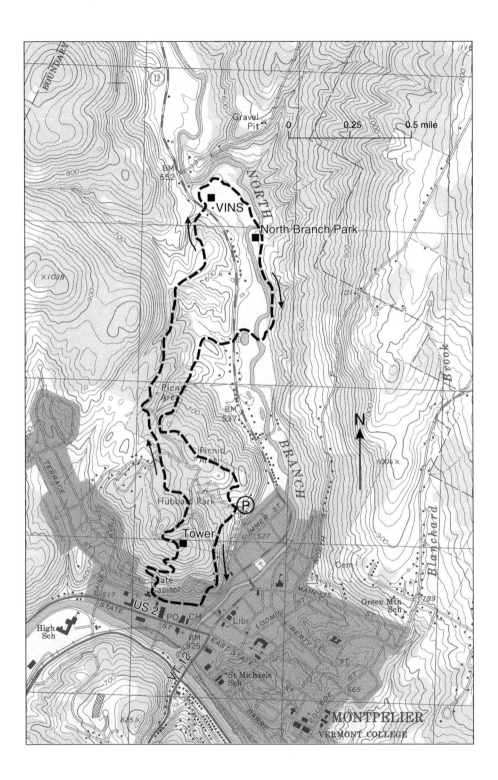

from the corner of State and Main in the center of the city, go 1 block west (toward the capitol building) on State Street, and turn right onto Elm Street at the court house. Follow Elm Street 0.3 mile, and turn left onto Winter Street. Follow Winter Street up a steep hill to the park gates. There is parking for about eight cars.

The Trail

From the park gates at Winter Road, walk past the FROG POND and over a small wooden bridge. Climb through the woods on a narrow path. Come to a four-way intersection of paths, and turn left. The path ends at a road. Turn left, and follow the road through the park gates. Continue downhill on Corse Street, a narrow, winding city street lined with old wooden houses. To the left is a view of downtown Montpelier: roofs and steeples nestled in a green valley formed by the Winooski and the North Branch Rivers. Downtown Montpelier is on the National Register of Historic Places as a well-preserved example of a typical 19th-century New England town. Turn left onto Cliff Street, then left again onto Hillside Avenue. Hillside soon ends at Court Street, which is a slightly larger street with a sidewalk. Turn right onto Court Street, follow it a few blocks until it ends, and turn right onto Greenwood Terrace. The golden dome of Vermont's state capitol building rises to your left. Continue straight up Greenwood Terrace, and enter the woods on a set of wide stone stairs. There is a sign that reads TOWER. The trail winds up a steep hill for just more than half a mile. Near the top of the climb, a number of smaller trails fan out to the sides, but stay on the main trail to reach the observation tower at the top of the hill.

The observation tower gives panoramic views of the mountains and valleys of central Vermont. It is said that on a clear day,

one can see seven mountain ranges. The tower was built over a period of 30 years using stone salvaged from old walls in the surrounding woods. It is made to have a "ruined castle" look, but is well maintained and it is safe to climb the staircase inside it!

In front of the tower is a gravel road. Facing the road, with your back to the tower, turn left onto the road and continue past a dozen large boulders lining the road. Pass a stone obelisk on the left side of the road. Come to a grassy area with a picnic table. Turn right off the road onto a narrow path in the woods. The trail descends into a ravine with sheer rock outcrops rising on both sides. Below the ravine, the trail junctions with a dirt road. Turn left, and follow the dirt road for just 100 feet. A footpath crosses the road. Turn left onto this path, and re-enter the woods. Several smaller paths branch off from the main footpath, but stay on the most obvious path that goes generally straight. After a while, the trail makes a sharp right and travels through a small bog on a narrow ridge of solid ground. Cross a dirt road, and continue on the footpath down a steep hill. A house is visible through the trees to the left. At the bottom of the hill, join Hubbard Park's Fitness Trail. The fitness trail is a series of exercise stations scattered through the park. Follow the posted instructions to test your strength and endurance against the likes of the ladder walk and the vault bar. Turn left, and cross a small wooden bridge. After a short way, the trail crosses a dirt road. Turn left onto the dirt road, and leave the fitness trail behind for now.

The dirt road ends in a cul-de-sac. There is an outhouse, grassy picnic area, and several stone fireplaces. Walk straight through the grassy area, and follow the footpath on the far side. Come to a four-way intersection of paths, and continue straight through.

The path quickly forks; go left. Starting here, the trail enters a deeryard. Dogs should be kept on a short leash here in the winter. The trail comes to a T-intersection near a brook; turn right. The trail forks again. Go left, following the sign to the nature center. After the sign, the trail goes over a small rise, then crosses a wooden bridge. The path diverges from the brook, climbing uphill (don't follow the faint path that parallels the brook). The path leaves the woods and enters a meadow. Enjoy views of forested hills to the north. The glimpses of a graveled area in the foreground is the Montpelier City Dump. The trail follows the crest of long, level hill with more good views to the east, then descends through the woods to City Dump Road.

Turn right on the road, and carefully cross VT 12 to the Vermont Institute of Natural Science (VINS). A small white house to the right is a nature center open to the public Monday through Friday, 9:00 A.M. to 5:00 P.M. A kiosk in the parking lot describes the self-guided nature trail on VINS property. Both VINS and North Branch Park are wildlife preserves, and hikers are asked to please leash their dogs. Turn left at the entrance to the VINS parking lot, and follow the rutted road around the edge of the large field. Pass a community garden and tree nursery, then follow along the edge of the North Branch River. Turn left across the river on a large steel bridge, and enter the city of Montpelier's North Branch Park. There is a blind on the left just past the bridge. Stand patiently in the blind to catch a glimpse of wildlife in the wetlands along the riverside. The trail follows a wide path through meadows and woods along the edge of the river. (Several other paths take off to the left and climb the forested hill. Please note that these paths do not all connect back to the main trail.) After about a quarter of a mile, take a hard right into a grassy recreation field with horseshoe pits and volleyball nets. Cross back over the river on a large wooden bridge, and enter a parking lot. Pass between the pool and the tennis courts. Follow around behind the white pool house, and climb up to VT 12 on the paved path.

Again, cross the road at the marked crosswalk, and continue up North Park Drive for a few hundred feet. The road bends left, and the hiking trail takes off to the right, descending through a field to a boardwalk, then climbing back into the woods and re-entering the boundaries of Hubbard Park. Take a left trail fork, then another left trail fork. At this second fork, the trail leaves behind the Hubbard Park deeryard (where dogs should be leashed in the winter). The trail winds through quiet woods along the edge of the park. At a four-way trail intersection, turn left. Reach a dirt road, and turn left. Follow the road 100 feet, and when the road bends right, follow the footpath that takes off to the left. Come to a T-intersection with another trail, and turn left again. Begin passing fitness trail exercise stations again. Enter a grassy area with a road and parking area to the right. This is a popular area for dogs to play and run free. Continue straight across the grass, and re-enter the woods on the footpath. When the trail forks, go left. The trail goes through rolling woodland, climbing and descending on wooden stairs. Smaller trails take off to each side, but stay on the most obvious trail. The trail skirts the edge of a meadow, with a picnic pavilion visible to the right. The meadow opens up to the left. Go down the hill through the meadow to the road. A mown path leads to the Winter Street park gate and your car in the parking area next to the Frog Pond.

45

Mount Hunger

Total distance: 4.4 miles

Hiking time: 3½ hours

Vertical rise: 2,290 feet

Rating: Moderately strenuous

Map: USGS 7.5' Stowe

This hike goes to the open south summit of Mount Hunger, which, at 3,539 feet, provides excellent views of the Green Mountain chain and the White Mountains of New Hampshire. Mount Hunger is part of the Worcester range, which begins near the Winooski River and ends at Elmore Mountain to the north.

How to Get There

From US2 in Waterbury, take VT 100 toward Waterbury Center, and turn east (0.0 mile) onto the road labeled WATERBURY CENTER P.O./LOOMIS HILL/BARNES HILL. This turn is south of the Cold Hollow Cider Mill, at a dip in the road opposite the Waterbury Reservoir Road. Drive straight 0.3 mile, and turn left (north) onto Maple Street. Just past the fire station, at 0.5 mile, turn right onto Loomis Hill Road, which turns to dirt at 2.4 miles. Bear left at the top of Loomis Hill Road, and continue on Loomis Hill Road until you reach a double parking area on your right at 3.9 miles. A sign at the second parking area identifies the trailhead for the WATERBURY TRAIL TO HUNGER MOUNTAIN, which is also the site where stones were crushed during construction of the interstate highway.

The Trail

Your pathway begins behind the parking areas and passes through the remains of the crusher site. There are no blazes at this point, but the trail is obvious. Blue blazes appear as the trail enters the woods at the trail register and begins a series of switch-

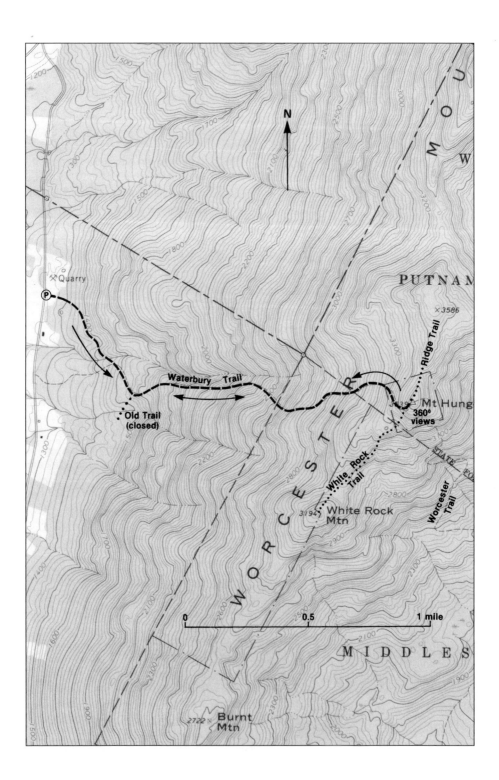

backs through huge, moss-covered boulders. Cross a small gully, and begin your climb along a side slope with numerous rock outcrops. At 0.5 mile, the trail levels, crosses a small brook, and resumes climbing along a moderate slope. At a second brook there is a partial view toward Camel's Hump.

Look for two large white birches, which indicate the end of the long hill. Turn right, and proceed along the hillside into a rock-strewn valley that provides cool, welcome relief on a hot summer day.

Look for a brook with a large boulder field upstream, which you will cross about 100 feet up from the left side. Continue uphill through birches until you meet an old trail at 1.0 mile on the right. Turn left up the hillside, with several views back into the valley. You soon cross another brook and enter a stand of white birches, much reduced by the January 1998 ice storm. Climb through rocks and roots until you find a nice flat rock on your left at 1.4 miles; this is a good place to sit and rest. The trail now enters a hemlock stand and becomes steeper as you pass over large rocks with limited views to the west. At 1.8 miles, you reach the junction of the White Rocks Trail, which branches to your right.

From the junction, continue on the main trail, which steeply ascends a short distance to a view of White Rock Mountain. As you near the summit, you scramble over rocks to the south summit of Mount Hunger. Stay on the rocks to avoid trampling the fragile alpine vegetation.

The south summit at 2.2 miles offers spectacular views of Waterbury Reservoir, Camel's Hump, White Rock Mountain, Mount Mansfield, the White Mountains, the Worcester Mountain Range, and area valleys. Enjoy the patterns created by the roads, fields, forests, ponds, and rivers below you.

As you prepare to return, be sure to avoid the blue-blazed Middlesex Trail, which descends to the other side of Hunger Mountain; another trail, the Skyline Trail, heads to the northern end of the Worcester range.

On the way back to your car, take time to admire the many stone steps and water bars built by Vermont Youth Conservation Corps trail crews to protect the trail bed. Like many Vermont mountain trails, this trail is subject to wear by hikers' boots and erosion by water.

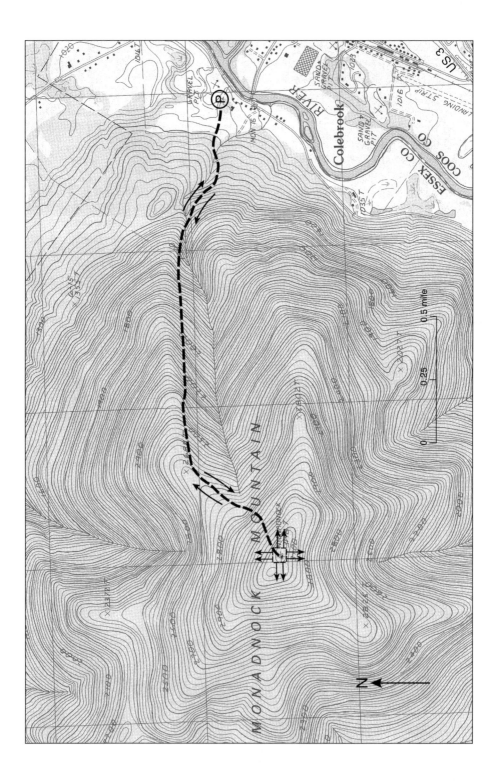

46

Mount Monadnock

Total distance: 4.8 miles

Hiking time: 4 hours

Vertical rise: 2,108 feet

Map: USGS 7.5' Monadnock Mountain, VT–NH

How big is the Northeast Kingdom? If you start from Hardwick, in the southeast corner, it will take you a good two hours by car to reach Monadnock in the northeast, in tiny Lemington. As a result, few hikers climb this mountain. Its peak is at 3,140 feet, and an abandoned fire tower caps the summit. There are no views until you reach the top, and even then, you'll need to struggle up the remains of the tower (currently missing its first few steps as well as some platforms) to get the real vista. Looking out over two states and Canada, though, makes the work well worthwhile.

Confusing this peak with the more famous one of the same name in southwestern New Hampshire is understandable. After all, the New Hampshire version actually gave its name, in 1893, to the newly recognized geological form. A monadnock is a conspicuous hill on a peneplain—an area of land that has reached geological "old age." This one has always been the center of Lemington life, and its forested slopes bear evidence of multiple loggings, as well as a long-vanished gold mine. A century ago, the trail up the mountain was a recognized town road (and the spur to the gold mine used often). Today it's a rugged, tree-enclosed route that has become a minor streambed, rocky and often wet. Summer wildflowers abound (in June, expect dogtooth violets, bunchberry blossoms, trillium in its deep red fullness, and clintonia). In late July, the blackberries at the base begin to yield fruit.

The trail is open for public use through

the courtesy of a paper company realty firm. Please respect this private property. The parking area and trailhead are well marked, and the trail up the mountain is plain (and blazed in yellow arrows), but there is a strip of trail between the gravel pit and the forest that's less obvious. Look for trampled grass, and if worse comes to worst, work upward from the snowmobile marker at the foot of the mountain.

The Connecticut River lies at the mountain's eastern foot; the mountain's southwestern extent reaches the former Champion Lands, now open to public access under careful rules to preserve its diversity of wildlife and rustic demeanor. A rail trail from the Ethan Allen plant in Canaan, north of the mountain, is expected to reach it at some point. Expect changes in access as the region shifts from mostly farming and logging to more specific recreation opportunities in the decade ahead.

How to Get There

Take VT 102 up the east side of Vermont along the Connecticut River from Bloomfield, passing through Lemington. North of the village, note the bridge on your right across the river to Colebrook. There is some parking by the bridge, good for larger groups. Trailhead parking is 0.2 mile north of the bridge at the gravel pit on the west side of VT 102. Enter the gravel pit, and park to the left, well out of the way of town machinery. Follow the wooden signs to the trail.

The parking area can easily host four to six cars at the left side of the pit. There are no facilities or safe water sources. Hiking boots are advisable, rather than sneakers, as the trail is mostly rocky. Until the fire tower is repaired, this is probably not a good trail for children, as the climb up the rickety tower is necessary to obtain any views along this hike.

The Trail

Follow the wooden signs from the parking area to the trailhead, up the sandbank on the left, to the fence line. Bear northeast along the edge of the field to the opening in the trees. You are entering a delicate glade of young hardwoods, berry bushes, and ferns. Yellow markers fastened to trees mark the route from here. The trail drops down slightly into a damp rill. Primitive handrails guide you beside massive, sweating stones, and at 0.8 mile, you cross the stream. Soon join a woods road, which you follow to the right. Be sure to pause here and look back down the mountain; this old woods road also descends the mountain, and you want to be sure to not take it as you return. At present a dropped birch trunk and a pile of stones serve as reminders to downhill hikers to cross the stream.

You follow the stream nearly all the way to the summit. The rise is steady and steep, decked with wildflowers. Note the relatively young trees of similar age, indicating logging that took place some 30 years back. Some small tree harvests have taken place more recently, and there are landings where the logs were gathered along this route.

Other travelers along the trail include deer (especially at the low part) and moose (mostly higher up). Each muddy area is likely to show tracks. Watch also for moose droppings, half an inch or more in diameter and rounded. Their saucer-sized hoofprints reveal their presence, maybe just minutes before you.

Birds along the trail include warblers, thrushes, partridge (ruffed grouse), and ravens. Hunting hawks circle overhead. Field guides to flowers, trees, and birds will enliven the steady, viewless climb.

After crossing a bridge over the stream at 1.8 miles near a small waterfall, the trail hugs the brook, then bears to the right to drier footing along a shoulder of the mountain. A gentle easing of undergrowth as the tree cover shifts to softwoods, with spruce and fir, can fool you into thinking the summit is just ahead, but you still have a good climb, working up the rocky turf and through some wet spots. Look back over your left shoulder often, though, to catch glimpses of the Connecticut River Valley as you near the top.

Keep an ear and eye out for birds as you move from the trail into the summit area with its tower; spruce grouse, considered rare, reside nearby. The tower, at 2.4 miles, is an irresistible climb and not difficult for those who like heights. Note that there are steps and pieces of platform missing. Even on a hot day, there's a stiff wind at the top of the tower, offering freedom from the blackflies that plague the damp trail. Beyond the tower a short path leads to the foundation of the fire lookout's cabin, with its isolated stone chimney still standing.

Return to the trail and hike back down, making sure to watch for the second crossing of the brook. *Note:* Don't expect to save much time on the descent, as the rounded stones along the way are slippery underfoot.

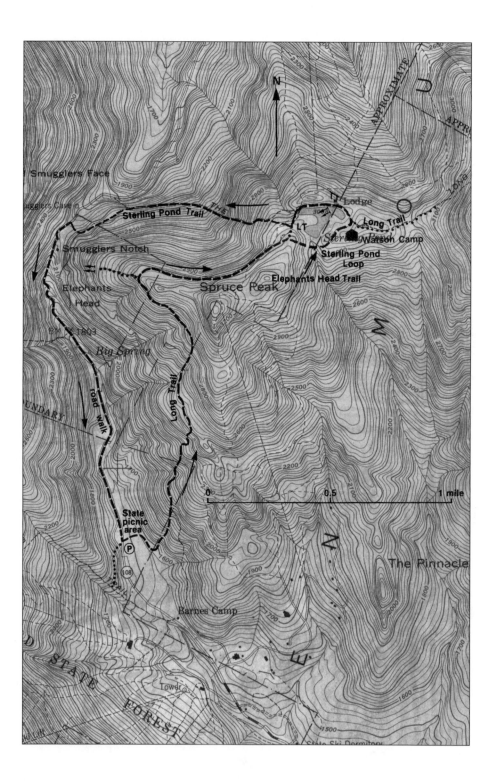

47

Sterling Pond and Elephant's Head

Total distance: 6.8-mile loop

Hiking time: 4½ hours

Vertical rise: 1,780 feet

Rating: Strenuous

Map: USGS 7.5' Mount Mansfield

This trail begins at the lower portion of Smugglers' Notch, a beautiful passageway between Mount Mansfield and Sterling Peak and a once-favorite route for smuggling goods into and out of Canada. In 1807, northern Vermonters faced a serious hardship when President Jefferson passed an embargo act, which forbade American trade with Great Britain and Canada. With Montreal such a close and lucrative market, however, many Vermonters continued illegal trade with Canada by herding cattle and transporting other goods through the notch. In the mid-1800s, fugitive slaves used the notch as an escape route to Canada. In the 1920s and 1930s, the notch was once again used to smuggle liquor from Canada during Prohibition.

Geologists date the rocks of the notch from about 400 million years ago. Today's rocks—originally the bottom of a shallow sea—contain clay particles, sand, and animal shells deposited on the sea floor. Over time, pressure from the ocean above pressed these particles into shale-type rocks. About 100 million years later, an uplift pushed up the sea floor and created the Green Mountains. When subjected to tremendous pressure and high temperatures associated with the uplift, these sedimentary rocks rearranged the minerals into the banded patterns seen today. This "metamorphosed" rock, called schist, primarily contains the minerals mica, albite, and quartz and occasionally garnet, magnetite, and chlorite.

Although uncertain about the formation

of the notch, most geologists believe that a southward-flowing river carved it. They speculate that as the first glacier retreated 12,000 years ago, ice on the eastern (warmer) side of the Green Mountains probably melted first. On the western (colder) side, the glacier continued to block any westward-flowing meltwater. Over time, a river of melted ice rushed through the path of least resistance—the notch—and down into the valley where Stowe is located today.

This geologic activity carved the magnificent cliffs of the notch into shapes resembling people or animals. Our forebears named them the Smuggler's Face, Singing Bird, Elephant's Head, and Hunter and His Dog. The cliffs also contain some of the rarest and most endangered plants in Vermont. Water, constantly dripping in the cliff's cracks, breaks down the rock minerals and nourishes the few plants that manage to grow on the outcroppings. Other factors—such as a steep face where few plants can survive, a cold microclimate, and a constant supply of mineral-rich water—combine to form an unusual plant environment, called a "cold calcareous cliff community." Please take extreme care to neither disturb nor pick any plants in the notch.

How to Get There
To reach the trail, take VT 108 (the Mountain Road) to the Smugglers' Notch Picnic Area parking lot on the north side of the highway. The 10- to 15-car parking lot is 0.8 mile from the Mount Mansfield Ski Area, 8.6 miles north of Stowe or 9.4 miles south of Jeffersonville.

The Trail
A 2002 relocation of the Long Trail (LT) replaced the road walk through Smugglers' Notch with a climb over Elephant's Head.

This hike follows the LT north to the Spruce Peak Ski Area. It continues north on the Elephant's Head Trail, circling Sterling Pond before rejoining the LT at the Sterling Pond Shelter. It then turns south, crossing several ski lift areas and descending to the Sterling Pond Trail (the route of the LT until the 2002 relocation). The ascent provides views of the ski slopes and summit of Mount Mansfield, and Taft Lodge, the largest of the LT shelters. A spur offers views from the top of the notch, and the hike concludes with a road walk through the base of the notch. This road walk can be eliminated if you have a second car to spot at the top of the notch, 1.3 miles north of the picnic area.

This strenuous hike—particularly the Elephant's Head section—requires crossing often-slippery rock ledge, scrambling over rock slides, and sometimes traversing the hillside using handholds provided by exposed rocks and roots. Although definitely not a technical climb, it requires some physical effort and demands proper equipment and preparation. Think carefully about starting this hike late in the day or if poor weather threatens.

Begin hiking after signing in at the trail register located at the east end of the Smugglers' Notch Picnic Area (0.0 mile). The trail crosses a small footbridge, turns left immediately before a closed log structure, and descends to a ford of the West Branch (during the spring or at other times of high water, you may need to detour upstream to find a suitable crossing).

After crossing a smaller stream, bear right, and ascend a long grade through a beech and birch forest, with intermixed fir trees and hobble bush. On the right, look for several dead trees. Beavers dammed the brook, creating a small pond that drowned the trees.

The trail bears away from the stream and

Sterling Pond

ascends in a series of switchbacks, with rock steps in—and several large downed trees around—the path. The trail levels out slightly before reaching a series of often-slippery rock ledges (0.7 mile), with seasonal flows of water crossing the path. Continue uphill on moderate grades through a mixed forest of birch and maple. At 1.5 miles, cross the lower portion of a 1985 rock and mud slide. Climb over several wet and mossy rocks, and enter a boreal forest dominated by coniferous trees (spruce, fir, and pine) with intermixed birch trees. The trail climbs steadily, parallel to the slide. It crosses a second slide at 1.7 miles. This area of loose scree rock and a garage-size boulder makes a good rest stop, with the ski slopes of Mount Mansfield, Adam's Apple, and the Chin visible across the notch.

The trail gets progressively rougher; you may need to use exposed roots and rocks as handholds to make progress up the mountain. Take care with your footing as you climb over several rock outcrops. Although rugged, this trail offers a great deal of satisfaction and unique views of the notch and surrounding cliffs.

The trail levels out slightly (2.0 miles), crosses a small stream, and reaches a flat spot above the second slide with views across the notch. Continue on the now-narrow tread way, across gulches filled with fallen trees and boggy areas, before reaching a spur to the left (2.5 miles).

Descend steeply left 300 yards on the spur to the top of the cliffs overlooking Smugglers' Notch. Looking 1,000 feet down into the notch, the road forms a horseshoe turn. When you reach the road walk at the end of your hike, use this turn as a marker to locate the cliffs. Across the road are the sheer walls of Mount Mansfield and the scar left by a 1983 landslide.

Peregrine falcons frequently nest around Smugglers' Notch, using thermals and wind currents to soar to the top of nearby peaks. In early spring, state naturalists evaluate the trails and locate any nesting sites, which sometimes requires closure of the Elephant's Head spur in order to protect these beautiful birds from disturbance. Please obey any trail signs during nesting season (February through mid-July; the introduction contains additional information about falcons).

Return to the main trail, and resume hiking north. The trail crosses several boggy areas and ascends steeply to a saddle just below Spruce Mountain. The trail continues to level and climb until it reaches Snuffy's Trail (3.0 miles), a rough road that connects the Spruce Peak Ski Area and Sterling Pond.

At this point, the LT turns westward (left) toward the Sterling Pond Trail, offering you an option:

To shorten the hike and return to VT 108, follow the LT as it descends along Snuffy's Trail and reaches a junction with the Sterling Pond Trail in 0.3 mile. You may descend farther along the LT and reach the outlook of Sterling Pond or follow the Sterling Pond Trail south 1.2 miles to the highway.

To continue the loop hike, cross Snuffy's Trail, and follow the blue-blazed Elephant's Head Trail. Descend a knoll through the spruce/fir forest, passing through some wet areas, rock outcroppings, and a cavelike opening around Sterling Pond.

The shallow, spring-fed Sterling Pond contains stocked trout; beavers frequently construct dams near the outlet. The pond formed after the last glacier cut a depression in a large talc deposit. Talc, a fine-grained mineral used in talcum powder and as a paper coating, feels soft and soapy, and makes certain stones extremely slippery along the tread way. Use caution when circling the pond. Only the remoteness of the pond saved it from development as a talc mine.

Pass Watson Camp, and ascend to a junction returning you to the LT at the north end of Sterling Pond. Now follow the LT south past Sterling Pond Shelter and along the ridge to the west of the pond. Cross under a ski lift line, and re-enter the woods. Descend on a steep wooden staircase overlooking the pond's outlet. The view north across the pond includes Madonna Mountain. Cross the outlet on puncheon, and ascend the ski trail connecting the Sterling and Spruce Peak lifts. At 5.0 miles, reach a junction with the Sterling Pond Trail, formerly the LT. (The white-blazed LT continues south and east to reach the junction with the Elephant's Head Trail.)

Now follow the blue-blazed Sterling Pond Trail south through a series of plateaus with occasional views, and descend on steep grades into Smugglers' Notch. Streams and rivulets frequently cross the trail. Rock steps, installed by the Long Trail Patrol over the years, help minimize erosion from this water and protect the tread way.

The trail continues to descend, with views into the western part of the notch. You begin to hear traffic noise when you reach the top of the cliff face and descend farther into the notch on a series of rock steps, along a plateau, and across a drainage gully.

Complete this section of the hike at the trail register at VT 108 (5.5 miles) at the height-of-land in Smugglers' Notch. During hiking season, the Vermont Agency of Natural Resources operates an information kiosk across the road from the register. A signboard explains some of the geology of the area and the smuggling that gave the notch its name. Behind the information kiosk is Smugglers' Cave, an alleged hiding place for contraband during the War of 1812.

From the trail register at VT 108, turn left (west), and carefully begin your roadside descent through the notch. This narrow, heavily used area brings motorized and human-powered vehicles into close proximity with hikers. Walk facing the traffic, and stay close to the edge of the road as you pass a series of large boulders (including King Rock, a large boulder that fell in 1910) and descend through several hairpin turns. Blue blazes indicate the direction on the road.

At the horseshoe bend, you might want to cross the road for a view of the Elephant's Head cliffs, where you viewed this road from the terminus of the spur trail several hours previously. Pass Big Spring (6.0 miles), the original location of a mountain hotel and a popular water source. Despite its scenic location, treat all water found in the woods before drinking. See the introduction for more information about waterborne diseases.

Continue descending on VT 108 until you reach the Smugglers' Notch Picnic Area and the LT trailhead register where you began your hike (6.8 miles).

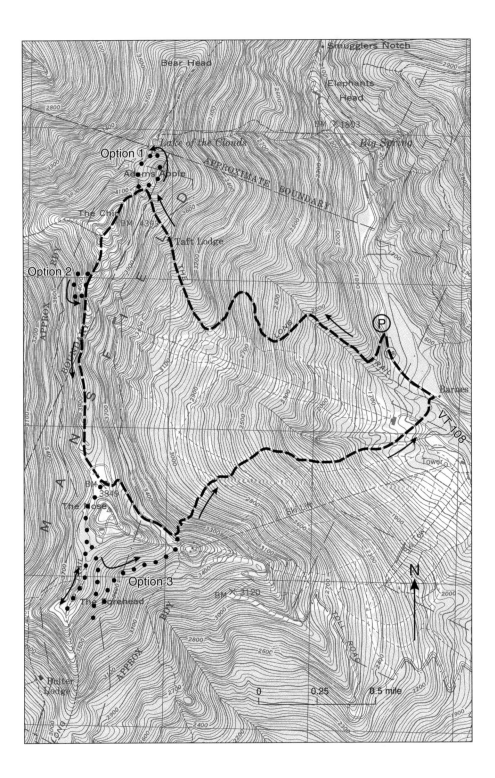

Bear Head

Smugglers Notch

Elephants Head

BM X 1803

Lake of the Clouds

Big Spring

Option 1

APPROXIMATE BOUNDARY

Adam's Apple

The Chin

BM X4393

D

Taft Lodge

Option 2

APPROX BDY

THE

LONG TRAIL

P

Barnes

VT 108

M A N S F I E L D

LONG TRAIL

Tower

BM 3849

Ski Lift

The Nose

APPROX BDY

Option 3

TOLL ROAD

N

The Forehead

BM X 3120

Butler Lodge

APPROX

LONG TRAIL

0   0.25   0.5 mile

48

Mount Mansfield

Total distance: 6.0 to 7.9 miles

Hiking time: 5 hours

Vertical rise: 3,200 feet

Rating: Difficult

Maps: USGS 7.5' Mansfield

With an elevation of 4,393 feet, Mount Mansfield ranks as the highest mountain in Vermont. The Abenaki called the mountain *Mose-o-de-be Wadso*, or "mountain-with-the-head-of-a-moose." Europeans probably named the mountain for the town of Mansfield, a mountain community disestablished in the mid-1800s. Today, the southern parts of the mountain are part of Underhill and Stowe, and the northern portion belongs to Cambridge.

This National Landmark resembles the profile of a human head with the body lying flat and looking up at the sky. From the east (Stowe) side, and traveling south to north on the ridge, observers can see the Forehead, Nose, Upper Lip, Lower Lip, Chin, and Adams Apple. Hikers using the following route climb Mount Mansfield from the east and reach the ridgeline at the Chin, then follow the summit ridge south.

The summit ridge of Mount Mansfield supports a rare and beautiful arctic-alpine plant community, notably sedges and heaths usually found a thousand miles north in the Canadian tundra. These fragile plants may resemble common grass and appear undistinguished, but you can help protect their fragile existence by avoiding them and staying on the trails and rock outcrops. The ridge of Mount Mansfield, owned by the University of Vermont, attracts more than 40,000 hikers each year and is included in the Vermont Fragile Areas Registry.

Through the cooperation of the University of Vermont, the Mount Mansfield Company, the Vermont Department of

Forests, Parks and Recreation, and the Green Mountain Club (GMC), summit caretakers provide detailed information about the alpine zone and its inhabitants during the hiking season. (See "Arctic-Alpine Vegetation" in the introduction.)

Visitors to the summit arrive by many routes, ranging from the direct, less demanding journey on the Toll Road to a ride on the gondola followed by a short, rugged hike (not recommended in wet weather) to the ridge and the Long Trail (LT). Hikers can choose from nine approach trails to the summit ridge, more than 15 other trails along the ridgeline, and 31 trails in the Mansfield area.

This hike follows the LT from VT 108 at Smugglers' Notch past Taft Lodge and climbs to the Chin. It continues on the LT to the summit station, where it descends via the Toll Road, Nose Dive Ski Trail, and Haselton Trail. This hike includes several options that allow you to view other points of interest, such as Adam's Apple, Lake of the Clouds, the Nose, and the Forehead. (Note that certain trails at the summit remain closed for ecological or safety reasons, among them the trail to Lake of the Clouds and to the Nose). As with any hike to the alpine zone, remember to bring warm clothing, rain gear, water, and a first-aid kit. The weather at the summit changes frequently and may not resemble the weather at the start of your hike.

How to Get There

Take VT 108 (the Mountain Road) to the LT parking area on the south side of the highway just before the Smugglers' Notch Picnic Area. Parking is available in a level area next to the road or along VT 108 shoulder. The 10- to 15-car parking lot is 0.7 mile from the Mount Mansfield Ski Area, 8.5 miles north of Stowe, or 9.5 miles south of Jeffersonville. Please do not block the road. If no parking spaces are available, park at the Mount Mansfield Ski Area Gondola Base Lodge and either walk to the LT trailhead or do the hike in reverse.

The Trail

A bulletin board at the LT trailhead on VT 108 contains current notices about safety and shelter availability on the trail. Make sure you sign the trail register, located about 50 yards from the road, which allows agencies to monitor trail use and confirm your presence on the mountain in event of an emergency.

Ascend the steep bank, hike parallel to the highway, and bear right on easier grades through a beech and yellow birch forest. Notice the extensive trail work of steps and water bars built over the years by the GMC to slow the impact of heavy trail use.

Follow the trail along a brook, then zigzag uphill. Bear right up a set of stairs, hike over rolling terrain, and cross a small brook twice. Continue your ascent with possible views of Elephant's Head, a great cliff on the east side of the notch.

A series of switchbacks ends at a rocky ledge (1.1 miles), with views of the Nose and summit towers. Bear right and ascend the sometimes steep trail. To your right you can see Spruce Peak Ski Area and Madonna Mountain. Begin a steady steep ascent. Follow the trail past the Hell Brook Cutoff and into a junction (1.7 miles). Directly ahead, the LT continues south to the Chin. A short trail to the right leads to a privy. To the left a spur leads to Taft Lodge. This log cabin, the largest and oldest shelter on the LT, dates from 1920. The GMC and other volunteers under the direction of Fred Gilbert rebuilt the lodge in 1996. It contains bunk space for 24 people, with a

Hikers approach the summit of Mount Mansfield

BILL CLARK

small fee charged for overnight use. A resident GMC caretaker stays at the lodge during the hiking season to assist hikers, maintain the local trails, and compost sewage to protect water quality. Because of the area's fragile nature, tent camping is not permitted, and there are special policies for waste disposal. Please follow all instructions while at the lodge.

Above Taft Lodge, follow the LT south past the junction with the Profanity Trail. This 0.5-mile-long trail, which connects Taft Lodge with the LT south of the Chin, offers a sheltered—but steep—alternate route to the ridge, especially in poor weather. It provides the option for a loop to the summit and a return to Taft Lodge.

Continue up the mountain through a field of ferns to a trail junction at Eagle Pass at 2.0 miles, where the LT, Adam's Apple Trail, and the Hell Brook Trail meet (see Option 1). Note that individuals with vertigo—and some pets—may find the route to the summit from Eagle Pass difficult. It also becomes quite slippery when wet. The Profanity Trail may be a more suitable route to the summit ridge.

From Eagle Pass, continue south on the LT, and ascend the steep face of the Chin to the summit of Mount Mansfield at 2.7 miles. Remember to stay on the marked trails and rock outcrops to avoid disturbing the fragile alpine vegetation and thin mountain soils. Many of these protected plants look like ordinary grass and are easily damaged by stray footsteps.

On a clear day, the Chin offers the following 360-degree views:

Northeast: The Sterling Range, Laraway Mountain, the Cold Hollow Mountains, Belvidere Mountain, Big Jay, Jay Peak, and the Pinnacle (in Canada).

East: The Worcester Mountain Range and, beyond them, the Granite Mountains and peaks of the Northeast Kingdom.

Southeast: Mount Washington in New

Hampshire and the White Mountains south of the Connecticut Lakes.

South: The Green Mountains to Killington Peak.

West: The Adirondack Mountains (New York), including Whiteface Mountain and Mount Marcy.

Northwest: Mount Royal (Canada) and the skyscrapers in Montreal.

After a rest to appreciate the spectacular view, continue south along the 2-mile ridgeline that connects the Chin with the Forehead. Hike past the Profanity and Sunset Ridge Trails to the junction of the Subway Trail at 3.0 miles on the west side of the ridge (see Option 2).

Continue along the ridgeline past a large rock cairn, Frenchman's Pile, the site where lightning struck and killed a hiker many years ago. If you are caught on the mountain during a thunderstorm, leave the ridge, and crouch upon loose rocks that are not immersed in standing water. Do not sit or lie upon the ground or touch the soil with your hands because ground currents may travel through your chest. Avoid exposed trees and rock outcrops. Caves and shallow overhangs are dangerous because ground currents jump through these gaps after a strike.

Descend along the ridge from the cairn. Stunted spruce and fir trees attest to the severity of the winter weather. Snow covers them during the winter, and wind and ice prevent normal growth. Although small, some of these trees may have survived 100 years. At this elevation, you can hear the distinctive musical call of the white-throated sparrow or the raucous cackling of ravens, or see an occasional peregrine falcon soaring on the thermals.

Stones on both sides of the footpath mark your route. In addition, the GMC-installed heavy timber bog bridges (called puncheon) as a footpath over some boggy areas. Remember to stay on the trail and protect this fragile ecosystem.

After crossing a gravel access road to the television towers, you reach the visitors center/summit station, where caretakers can answer your questions (see Option 3). A parking lot for the Toll Road sits below the summit station. The side trail to the Nose offers a parting look at the ridge you have just hiked.

The old Mount Mansfield Summit House, one of New England's most successful summit hotels until 1958, once occupied the land now devoted to the Toll Road parking lot. Writing about the Summit House on a visit in 1862, the poet and essayist Ralph Waldo Emerson wrote that "a man went through the house ringing a large bell and shouting 'Sunrise,'" every morning. Vigorous guests rolled out of bed and climbed the Nose for a prebreakfast view of the emerging dawn.

From the summit station, descend the Toll Road to the Nose Dive Ski Trail, a former ski racecourse. (A piped spring to the right of the road allows hikers to replenish their water supplies. Locals informally refer to this water source as the "runny nose." Water from this untested water source requires treatment before drinking.) Descend the ski trail (zig, zag, and zig), and look for a trail sign on the left for the Haselton Trail. This trail, one of the oldest on the mountain and the original route of the LT between the summit house and the Stowe Valley, is named for Judge Seneca Haselton, the first vice-president of the GMC.

The Haselton Trail leaves the ski trail, enters the woods to the left, and follows a brook downhill. The trail leaves the woods at the base of the mountain at a ski area service road immediately above the Midway Base Lodge parking lot. Pass under the gondola and in front of the Midway Lodge, cross another gravel service road, and reach the upper parking lot of the Mount Mansfield Ski Area and the Gondola Base Station at 4.4 miles. Follow the exit signs on the paved access road to VT 108, turn left, go past Barnes Camp (which once housed loggers working on the mountain and GMC seasonal staff), and walk on the road to your car (5.8 miles).

Options

Option 1: Adams Apple/Hell Brook Loop–Bear right at the junction on the Adams Apple Trail, and ascend to the open summit of the Adams Apple (elevation 4,060 feet). The steep wall of the Chin towers over the trail to the south. Continue north on the Adams Apple Trail toward Lake of the Clouds, the highest lake in Vermont. At the junction of the Hell Brook and Bear Pond Trails, turn left onto the Hell Brook Trail around the Adams Apple, and return to Eagle Pass. Total distance for this option: 0.3 additional mile.

Option 2: Subway–Although fun and exciting, the Subway Trail is extremely difficult. Avoid it when carrying a full backpack or in bad weather because the rocks become extremely slippery. The trail steeply descends the western face of the mountain through a rock fall area. Maneuvering around the caves, crevices, and boulders demands some agility. After passing through the Subway and ascending a ladder, return to the ridge on the Subway and Canyon North Extension Trail, a short distance from the starting point. Total distance for this option: 0.3 mile.

Option 3: The Forehead–Continue south on the LT from the visitors center. The trail emerges from the woods on the gravel service road and passes the blue-blazed Lakeview Trail. Stay on the road, and follow the LT (south) when it leaves the road to the right and enters the woods. Pass the Forehead Bypass, an alternate route for LT hikers in severe weather, and continue south on the LT to a junction with the Wampahoofus Trail on the open summit of the Forehead (elevation 3,940 feet). Return to the Forehead Bypass, and follow it downhill for 0.3 mile, sometimes on steep rock slabs, to the South Link. Turn left, and follow the South Link on a rough, rocky way across the south end of the mountain to the Toll Road parking lot across from the Nose Dive. Resume your descent down the Nose Dive to the Haselton Trail. Total distance for this option: 1.3 additional miles.

49

Camel's Hump

Total distance: 7.4 miles

Hiking time: 6 hours

Vertical rise: 2,645 feet

Rating: Strenuous

Maps: USGS 7.5' Waterbury; 7.5' Huntington

This challenging hike takes you to the 4,083-foot summit of Camel's Hump through a low-elevation forest dominated by birch, beech, and maple; then a boreal (spruce/fir) forest at higher elevations; and ultimately an alpine plant community at the summit. Rushing streams, beaver ponds, and many impressive views give way to scree rock and boulders ground by glacial action before you climb to the summit cone of Camel's Hump. One of several routes to the summit, the Monroe/Dean/Long Trail loop offers an exciting and picturesque opportunity to see mountain ecosystems merge into Arctic-like alpine areas within the space of a few miles.

The Waubawakee Indians called Camel's Hump *Tawabodi-e-wadso*, which means "the saddle mountain." Legend says that Samuel de Champlain's explorers thought the mountain looked like a resting lion and so called it *le lion couchant*, or "the couching lion." In 1798, Ira Allen referred to the mountain as Camel's Rump on a historical map. From that name, Zadock Thompson in 1830 called the mountain Camel's Hump.

During the Civil War, Camel's Hump served as a well-known resort with horse and carriage trails leading to guest houses at the base and summit. Its popularity waned, however, with competition from the Mount Mansfield resort complex. In the early 1900s, area businessmen restored the trails and the summit house. Later, Professor Will Monroe of the Couching Lion Farm (the trailhead of this hike) continued

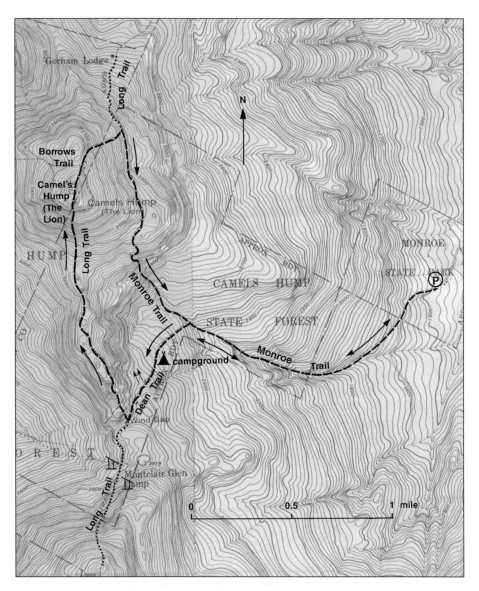

these efforts by developing a section of the Long Trail (LT) named the Monroe Skyline.

In 1911, Colonel Joseph Battell gave 1,000 acres of land, including Camel's Hump, to the state of Vermont for one dollar, specifying that the entire forest be "preserved in a primeval state." The summit and surrounding state land became a Natural Area in 1965, and the National Park Service designated Camel's Hump a Registered National Natural Landmark in 1968. The Camel's Hump State Forest, established by the Vermont legislature in 1969, includes all lands extending from VT 17 north to the Winooski River and from the Huntington River to the Mad River. The forest now in-

---

BILL CLARK

The view from the summit of Camel's Hump

cludes nearly 24,000 acres of land.

As one of the highest backcountry use areas in Vermont, Camel's Hump averages 10,000 to 15,000 visitors a year, primarily day hikers. The volume of traffic widens the pathway and demands extensive and difficult trail maintenance to accommodate the heavy foot traffic.

Protecting the summit's fragile arctic-alpine vegetation remains a high priority. Those "fields of grass" on the summit are actually rare and endangered tundra species limited to an area of approximately 10 acres on the summit (Mount Mansfield supports the largest tundra in Vermont, about 250 acres on the ridgeline). Because excessive trampling of plants and soil leads to loss of rare vegetation and precious soil necessary for regeneration, walk only on marked trails and rock outcrops. Green Mountain Club (GMC) summit caretakers, on duty during the hiking season, assist hikers and explain the fragile nature of this en-

vironment. All visitors can help by following their instructions. The introduction contains additional information about this unique plant community in the "Arctic-Alpine Vegetation" sectionof the introduction.

How to Get There

Begin at the junction of US 2 and VT 100 just off exit 10 of I-89 (0.0 mile) in Waterbury. Drive south on VT 100, and pass under a railroad trestle with playing fields to the right. At 0.1 mile, turn right onto Winooski Street, cross the Winooski Street bridge, and immediately turn right onto River Road (0.4 mile). At 5.0 miles, turn left (south) onto Camel's Hump Road. Several side roads branch off the Hump Road; stay on the main road. At 6.4 miles, bear left at the fork, and cross the bridge. Continue across another bridge and past a sign that reads WELCOME TO CAMEL'S HUMP STATE PARK. A side road to the left leads to parking for the Camel's Hump View Trail, which also serves as the winter parking lot and over-flow summer lot. Pass the last year-round residence to the right, and drive up the rough, steep, narrow road to the summer parking lots. On the right at 8.5 miles, opposite a gated road, is a large parking area with space for 20 to 25 cars. The road ends at 8.7 miles in the Couching Lion Farm parking area with space for an additional 20 to 25 cars.

Emergency vehicles, residents, and other cars require access to the trailhead, so please avoid blocking the gated road, and do not park on the shoulders of this narrow road.

The Trail

Follow the blue-blazed trail from the parking area into the woods. Pass a water source on the left and a memorial to American service personnel killed in a 1944 crash of a B-24 bomber near the summit. Continue past the composting privy on the right, and reach a trail registration box and information board. A trail map shows the several trails used during this loop hike, and the bulletin board contains displays about natural history subjects. Sign in at the registration box, then follow the blue-blazed Monroe Trail.

The forest here is composed of mixed spruce and fir, with beech, birch, oak, and maple trees common. Ferns, moss, and lichen grow in the wetter areas along the trail. Early morning is a good time to hear thrushes and song sparrows. Shortly after leaving the registration box, cross the first of three footbridges. Cross the third footbridge at 0.8 mile, and climb to a trail junction at 1.3 miles. Take the left fork, and follow the Dean Trail, a narrow, less-traveled path that offers a pleasant forest walk with views of several streams, ponds, and the summit. The Monroe Trail, on which you

will return, bears right. Descend to a footbridge built by the Youth Conservation Corps in 1991, crossing Hump Brook at 1.5 miles. Then pass a spur to the left leading to Hump Brook Tenting Area, a popular primitive campsite. Continue uphill, cross a birch-covered knob at 2.0 miles, and reach a spur to a view of Camel's Hump over a beaver pond.

The trail climbs steadily past several glacial erratics—large boulders moved by glacial action—and through a notch to the LT at Wind Gap. A sharp left turn takes you on the original route of the LT, now the Allis Trail. Straight ahead the LT leads 0.2 mile south to Montclair Glen Lodge, a log and frame trail cabin built in 1948 by the Long Trail Patrol. A GMC caretaker resides here during the hiking season, with a small fee charged for overnight use.

Turn right to follow the white-blazed LT north. Carefully climb the steep ledges past the rock face overlooking the beaver pond. From the top of the rock face, you can see the pond and valley below and Mount Ethan Allen to the south. The trail climbs along the rock outcrop, enters a cleft in the rock at 2.6 miles, and reaches an overlook. Ascend another knob, and enjoy the view of Camel's Hump's summit. Wild blueberries line the trail, giving late summer hikers an unexpected treat.

As you descend toward the west side of the ridge, the forest becomes more dense with spruce and fir trees, and the temperature cools as you pass through some boggy areas. The trail drops into the col and then ascends again at 3.4 miles. This steep traverse of the southwest face of the mountain also provides several views of the summit. At 3.8 miles you reach the Alpine Trail junction, a yellow-blazed trail that circles the summit to the east and provides a bypass in bad weather. Continue north on

---

Camel's Hump

the LT, over the exposed western face of the Hump, and reach the 4,083-foot summit at 4.0 miles. Remember the fragile nature of this summit area, and stay on the marked trails and rock outcrops. Help to protect this rare and endangered ecosystem.

From the summit you can hear white-throated sparrows and see juncos, ravens, and possibly peregrine falcons, as well as some spectacular views on a clear day:

North: Mount Mansfield, Belvidere Mountain with the white scar of its asbestos mine, and Owl's Head in Canada.

South: Mounts Ethan and Ira Allen, Lincoln Ridge with wide ski trails, and Killington and Pico Peaks.

East: The Worcester Mountain Range, Barre's Granite Mountains, and the White Mountains of New Hampshire, including Mount Washington, the Presidential Range, Mount Moosilauke, and the Franconia Range.

West: The Champlain Valley and New York's Adirondack Mountains, including Whiteface Mountain standing alone to the north.

After resting to enjoy the scenery and eat lunch, follow the white blazes north across the summit on the LT. Descend on the rocky trail to the hut clearing (4.3 miles), the original site of a summit house in the mid-1800s and three tin-roofed shelters from 1912 to the 1950s. A caretaker stayed in one hut; the others provided separate lodging for men and women.

Three trails diverge at the hut clearing: The Burrough's Trail descends west 2.1 miles to Huntington Center. The LT continues north to the Winooski River along Bamforth Ridge. The Monroe Trail leads east to Couching Lion Farm and your car, a distance of 3.1 miles.

Follow the blue-blazed Monroe Trail downhill, reaching the yellow-blazed Alpine Trail at 4.9 miles. Continue to descend the Monroe Trail's ledges through mixed hard- and softwoods. Cross Camel's Hump Brook at 5.2 miles, and soon walk along the base of a large rock face. At 5.4 miles, you descend a birch-gladed ridge, then hike over rocks that have fallen from the outcrop above you. At 6.1 miles, reach the Monroe/Dean Trail junction, and complete your loop. Continue downhill to the parking area at 7.4 miles.

Note: Older maps and guidebooks may list the Monroe Trail as the Forestry Trail. The name change in 1997 to the Monroe Trail honors Will S. Monroe, a legendary LT pioneer and trail builder.

50

Hazen's Notch to Eden Crossing

Total distance: 10.0 miles

Hiking time: 1½ days, 1 night

Vertical rise: 3,043 feet

Rating: Strenuous

Map: USGS 7.5' Hazens Notch

The Long Trail (LT) between VT 58 at Hazen's Notch and VT 118 at Eden Crossing features steep climbs and rewarding views of the mountains of northern Vermont. The main feature of this portion of trail is Belvidere Mountain, famous for its now-defunct asbestos mines and fire tower.

The acquisition of 1,946 acres of land, including the summits of Belvidere Mountain, Haystack Mountain, and Tillotson Peak, was the Green Mountain Club (GMC)'s first major land purchase in its Long Trail Protection Campaign in northern Vermont. This valuable property includes 3 miles of the LT, 4 miles of side trails, Tillotson Camp, and Lockwood Pond. The purchase has allowed the GMC to both protect valuable natural and trail resources and move toward its overall goal of creating a protected corridor for the entire LT.

How to Get There

Spot a car at the LT parking area on VT 118, 4.8 miles west of VT 100 in Eden and 6.1 miles east of VT 109 in Belvidere Center. The parking area is located off the north side of the road a short distance west of the LT crossing.

After spotting one car, return to VT 100, and travel north 10 miles to the village of Lowell and the junction with VT 58. After 2 miles, VT 58 becomes a dirt road and begins its climb into Hazen's Notch. Close to the height-of-land (5.5 miles), there is a small pull-off area for cars on the south side of the road.

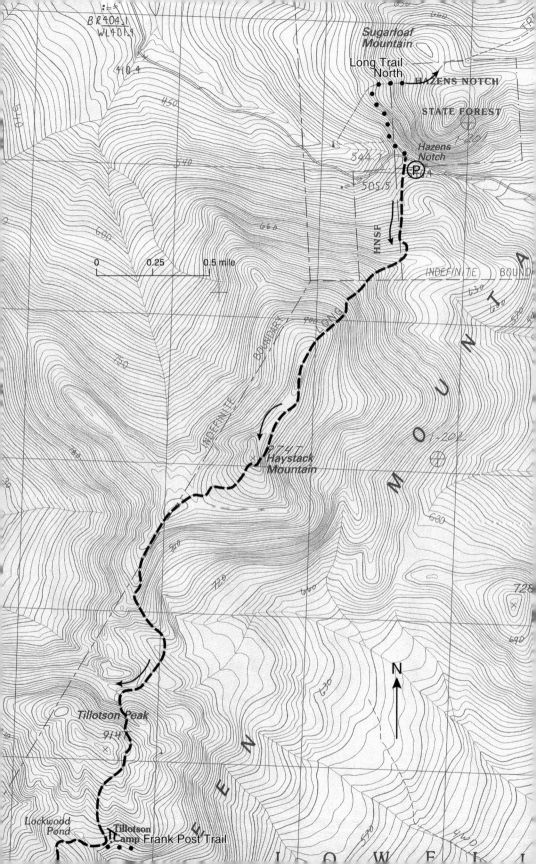

The Trail

Day One

Total distance: 4.6 miles
Hiking time: 4½ hours
Vertical rise: 2,243 feet

The LT leaves the road just east of the height-of-land. Look for a nearby granite marker designating the site as the North Terminus of the Bayley-Hazen Road. This road was built for military purposes in the late 1700s and was originally intended to stretch from Peacham, Vermont, to the Canadian border. To the north, the cliffs of Sugarloaf Mountain loom nearly 700 vertical feet above the road's high point.

Take the white-blazed LT south, which enters the woods and immediately begins to climb. Leaving Hazen's Notch, the trail ascends steeply up the north side of Haystack Mountain. Most of the elevation is gained within the first mile as the trail climbs along rock faces that are often wet and slippery. Proceed with caution, and pause often to watch the notch extend below you. The trail becomes more moderate at 1.0 mile but continues along rugged rocky terrain to the top of Haystack Mountain. At 1.9 miles, the LT reaches a spur that leads you west to the true summit. Drop your pack, and make the worthwhile 0.2-mile jaunt out to the boreal-forested summit, with views of Hazen's Notch and Jay Peak to the north. After the quick side trip, proceed downhill off the south side of Haystack Mountain. For the next 2 miles, the trail follows a moderate grade as it passes through numerous wet spots and up and over a number of lesser knobs. Moving in and out of mixed hardwoods, the trail approaches the base of Tillotson Peak by first crossing a small stream. The ascent is a short affair, climbing several rock outcroppings and sturdy rock staircases. At 4.1 miles, the trail passes east of Tillotson's summit and makes a quick descent to the Frank Post Trail, leading 50 feet east to Tillotson Camp (4.6 miles).

Tillotson Camp, built in 1939, is a frame cabin with bunk space for eight. The camp has a large front window that can be opened (carefully!) to excellent views of Eden and glimpses of the asbestos mines below. The now-closed asbestos mines of Eden Mills once produced more than 60 percent of the world's supply of long-fiber asbestos. In nice weather, the rocks in front of the cabin offer a sunny spot for relaxing and cooking dinner. A reliable stream flows 100 feet to the north behind the cabin on the Frank Post Trail. The outhouse is located 50 feet south on the LT.

Day Two

Total distance: 5.4 miles
Hiking time: 3½ hours
Vertical rise: 800 feet

Leaving the shelter, follow the white-blazed LT south to the left of the shelter. This area is quite wet. Watch for moose tracks as you cross the outlet of the beaver pond. You soon reach Lockwood Pond. This high-elevation pond, a subalpine tarn, forms the headwaters of the Missisquoi River, which flows north into Canada.

The LT skirts the southern edge of the pond until it begins a steady climb away from the pond at 0.5 mile. Look behind you for good views of yesterday's hike. Follow the ridgeline up, down, and across numerous plateaus. Be careful in this section because the trail is frequently wet and slippery. Along this section of trail, the remnants of Hurricane Floyd nearly swept the ridge clear of trees, especially near the Belvidere saddle. GMC volunteers put in many hours to make this section passable in the fall of 1999. At 2.8 miles, you reach the

Lockwood Pond

junction with the Forester's Trail. At this junction, follow the blue-blazed summit spur 0.2 mile up to the Belvidere fire tower.

In 1919, a summit lookout station was established with the construction of a cabin, telephone lines, tower, and trail. In 1938, a hurricane blew down the old tower, and a new steel tower was built. In 1968, a new trailer-type cabin was airlifted by helicopter to the summit. The tower was operated until about 1970, when airplane patrols replaced many fire towers. The current tower was renovated into a public lookout tower by the GMC in 1992.

From the tower there are excellent views: To the north, the previous day's summits, Tillotson Peak and Haystack Mountain, are in the foreground; the summit station on Jay Peak is directly behind Haystack, with Little Jay to the left; to the east, you can see the entire White Mountain range, from Mount Moosilauke in the south to the Presidentials in the north; to the southeast are Lake Eden, Green River Reservoir, and the Worcester Mountain Range from Mount Hunger to Elmore Mountain; to the southwest is the Green Mountain range, including Mount Abraham, Camel's Hump, Mount Mansfield, Madonna Mountain, Whiteface Mountain, Butternut Mountain, and finally, Laraway Mountain; to the west are the nearby Cold Hollow Mountains and beyond, New York's Adirondack Mountains.

After enjoying the view, return to the junction with the Forester's Trail. From this junction, continue on the LT toward VT 118. Head south from the junction, traveling through a moss-covered fir forest stand until the trail begins to drop. The path becomes a bit of a scramble downhill on a variety of ledges. At 4.3 miles, the trail levels out somewhat as the terrain becomes more gradual, transitioning into a mixed forest of birch, beech, and maple. Cross a small stream at 5.2 miles, and descend to trailhead and your car (5.4 miles).

Index

G

H

N

Y